Cambridge Elements

Elements in Applied Linguistics
edited by
Li Wei
University College London
Zhu Hua
University College London

CRISIS LEADERSHIP

Boris Johnson and Political Persuasion during the Covid Pandemic

Philip Seargeant
Open University

CAMBRIDGE
UNIVERSITY PRESS

Shaftesbury Road, Cambridge CB2 8EA, United Kingdom

One Liberty Plaza, 20th Floor, New York, NY 10006, USA

477 Williamstown Road, Port Melbourne, VIC 3207, Australia

314–321, 3rd Floor, Plot 3, Splendor Forum, Jasola District Centre,
New Delhi – 110025, India

103 Penang Road, #05–06/07, Visioncrest Commercial, Singapore 238467

Cambridge University Press is part of Cambridge University Press & Assessment,
a department of the University of Cambridge.

We share the University's mission to contribute to society through the pursuit of
education, learning and research at the highest international levels of excellence.

www.cambridge.org
Information on this title: www.cambridge.org/9781009321976

DOI: 10.1017/9781009321983

First published 2023

A catalogue record for this publication is available from the British Library.

ISBN 978-1-009-32197-6 Paperback
ISSN 2633-5069 (online)
ISSN 2633-5050 (print)

Crisis Leadership

Boris Johnson and Political Persuasion during the Covid Pandemic

Elements in Applied Linguistics

DOI: 10.1017/9781009321983
First published online: February 2023

Philip Seargeant
Open University
Author for correspondence: Philip Seargeant, philip.seargeant@open.ac.uk

Abstract: This Element examines the way that Boris Johnson's government handled the early months of the Covid crisis in the UK, with a particular focus on the role of rhetoric and communication in enacting their leadership strategy. In liberal democracies, persuasive communication is a vital tool for the execution of power, and leadership is often seen to rely on effective communication practices. The Element focuses in particular on the ways in which notions of trust and authority were constructed as part of this strategy, and how these operated as key indexicals meant to provide a foundation for effective persuasion. It examines how, within a few weeks of the start of the lockdown policy, media opinion had begun opining that the government was losing the trust of the electorate due to actions related to this communications strategy, which had the effect of undermining its authority of influence.

Keywords: politics, leadership, propaganda, authority, political communication

ISBNs: 9781009321976 (PB), 9781009321983 (OC)
ISSNs: 2633-5069 (online), 2633-5050 (print)

Contents

1 Power with Responsibility

The Covid Era

The Covid crisis crept up on Europe at the beginning of 2020. The first recorded cases were in early December 2019 in Wuhan, Hubei, China. By the end of January 2020, cases were first being recorded in Italy (Severgnini, 2020). By June of that year, the UK had the highest number of Covid-related deaths in Europe and the third highest in the world (after the United States and Brazil).

After the first few months of the pandemic, a growing consensus had developed in the UK media and the scientific community that the government had been slow to react at the outset of the crisis, causing thousands of unnecessary deaths (e.g., Horti, 2020), and that what positive progress it did then achieve was undermined by a series of missteps and scandals which destabilised its messaging (Fancourt et al., 2020). This appeared to be reflected in public opinion as a 60-point drop in the government approval ratings for its handling of the crisis between March and June 2020 was recorded (Kellner, 2020). This book looks at these claims within the context of a discourse on political leadership. It looks at how the government was perceived as losing the trust of the electorate due to certain actions and decisions relating to its communications strategy (Bermingham, 2020), and how this in turn undermined its authority of influence and, ultimately, contributed to the downfall of the Prime Minister.

The arguments outlined here are based on two key premises: firstly, that communication is key to leadership and that effective leadership is, in great part, a product of a persuasive communicative strategy. And secondly, that persuasive communication for political leadership relies on *indexing* concepts of both authority and trust (Eglene et al., 2007; Hassan and Ahmed, 2011) which then contributes to the calibre of voice which imbues the government's message with its persuasive power. The concept of indexicality which I am using here is, in sociolinguistic or linguistic anthropological terms, the phenomenon by which language and other forms of semiosis generate contextual meaning by drawing upon the relationship between speech and certain ideologies within the culture (Silverstein, 1976, 2003). For instance, a particular accent may index for the listener a set of cultural prejudices which will influence how they interpret the message the speaker is trying to convey. Or a military commander may index their battlefield experience and thus martial expertise by displaying a chestful of medals. The UK government in the early stages of the Covid crisis, I will argue, sacrificed both trust and authority through decisions affecting the context underpinning the communication of their messaging, which ultimately stripped the communication – and thus the leadership – of much of its pragmatic effectiveness.

In other words, while they made every effort in their orchestrated acts of communication to index authority and trustworthiness, certain of the actions and behaviour they indulged in created a very different context for interpretation. In looking at this, I will consider the question of what an analysis of the government's communication strategy for the pandemic, and the way this was mediated by news organisations, can contribute to an understanding of leadership in a time of crisis.

The Engines of Propaganda

Just before the UK general election of 1931, the then Prime Minister Stanley Baldwin attacked the press in a speech, saying:

> The newspapers attacking me are not newspapers in the ordinary sense. They are engines of propaganda for the constantly changing policies, desires, personal vices, personal likes and dislikes of the [press barons]. What are their methods? Their methods are direct falsehoods, misrepresentation, half-truths, the alteration of the speaker's meaning by publishing a sentence apart from the context . . . What the proprietorship of these papers is aiming at is power, and power without responsibility – the prerogative of the harlot through the ages. (Quoted in Ball, 1988)

Jump forward almost a century, to two headlines from the British press for Wednesday, 13 April 2022. The *Mirror* runs with 'Led by Liars and Lawbreakers', with the subtitle 'First PM [prime minister] to break the law in office' (The Mirror, 2022). The *Daily Mail* goes with the strapline 'Boris [Johnson] was there for nine minutes. Carrie [Johnson] less than five. The birthday cake never left its Tupperware box. And last night the PM rightly apologised. As the Left howls for resignations over Met's £50 Covid fines . . .', followed by the main headline: 'Don't they know there's a war on?' (Daily Mail U.K., 2022).

These two front pages are reporting the same event – so-called 'partygate' – but doing so in ways which exemplify almost too dramatically the role played by discourse in construing the social world. The event in question here is the fining of the Prime Minister of the time, Boris Johnson, and his then Chancellor of the Exchequer, Rishi Sunak, for having broken the regulations against social gatherings in the early months of the coronavirus epidemic – regulations that their own government had put in place – by attending a party in the workplace. But not only had the Prime Minister broken these regulations, he had seemingly denied doing so in comments he made to parliament, and had thus, in effect, lied about his behaviour. This is succinctly expressed in the *Mirror* headline. The *Daily Mail*, on the other hand, a paper traditionally loyal to the Conservative

Party (of which Johnson was the leader), attempts to contextualise – and thus downplay – the offences through reference to the ongoing war in Ukraine.

The news media, in its conceptualisation as the Fourth Estate, likes to promote itself as a crucial means within society for holding power to account (Schultz, 1998). It operates as one of the checks and balances on governments in a liberal democracy. Political leaders, when the newspapers are strikingly critical of their actions and behaviour, tend to see things more in Stanley Baldwin's terms, and view the media somewhat less flatteringly. Thus it is that competing 'engines of propaganda' attempt to persuade public opinion, and accusations of 'direct falsehoods, misrepresentation [and] half-truths' are flung from one institution to the other.

The incident that the press rather unimaginatively termed 'partygate' was one in a long line of scandals which dogged Johnson's government's handling of the Covid pandemic and raised questions about the Prime Minister's leadership in a time of crisis. Debates over this were instigated and mediated by press coverage, with politicians attempting, at each stage, to manage the way their plans and actions were being portrayed by journalists (e.g., Fitzgerald, 2021).

With each scandal, there were certain reoccurring elements in the ensuing criticism which suggested a shape for what was understood within the media as competent and effective leadership and that indicated why the government was supposedly failing in this. Many of these elements – described and analysed below – had to do with the way that effective communication was seen as crucial for shepherding the population through the constantly shifting realities of living in a society suffering under a pandemic (Hyland-Wood et al., 2021).

By the time of the 'partygate' scandal (early 2022), the political context relating to the pandemic had changed somewhat from the earlier stages, and this had altered the implications over ministers' actions. In short, the situation shifted from a scenario which had both ethical *and* leadership-via-persuasion implications to one which was predominantly just ethical. The accusations faced by Johnson and Sunak were that they had flouted the very regulations they themselves had formulated and enacted into policy, and that Johnson had then lied to the House of Commons when he initially refuted these accusations (White, 2022). These are clearly serious ethical issues, and were framed by the government's critics as such, as can be seen in the headline from the *Mirror*.

By this stage, however, most of the regulations which had been put in place to contain the virus had now been abandoned, so criticism that the PM and Chancellor's actions undermined the message they were attempting to convey were far less prevalent than they had been earlier in the pandemic. Indeed, the pragmatic argument being employed by the PM's allies (such as the *Daily Mail*) in relation to the incident was that the geopolitical situation with respect to the war in Ukraine was such that it would be foolhardy to lose the leader of the country at this particular juncture. But prior to this, especially in those first few months after the virus had first surfaced and begun spreading, the issue of leadership-via-persuasion was central to discussions in the media about the conduct of the members of the government. The management of public opinion was seen as essential for guiding the nation through the crisis.

The Place of Persuasion in Liberal Democracy

On the day that lockdown restrictions were lifted in England in July 2021 there was a large anti-lockdown demonstration outside the Houses of Parliament in Westminster (Batchelor, 2021). The logic behind a crowd of people gathering to protest against something which had ceased that very day seemed a little confused, to say the least. But logic wasn't perhaps the guiding principle behind the demonstrators' actions. They were motivated more by conviction: the conviction that the entire Covid crisis had been manufactured – or, at the very least, exaggerated – by establishment agents as a way of curtailing the rightful liberties of everyday citizens (Özdüzen et al., 2021). The protesters subscribed to a number of conspiracy theories, all of which preached the same basic story that the severity of the virus had been fabricated by those in power as a way of further consolidating this power. The government, the medical profession and the media, all of whom worked for the establishment, were manipulating the fears and emotions of ordinary people by means of an invented scare story.

The story the demonstrators told themselves was not only delusional but, as with all conspiracy theories, it also relied on a very simplistic idea of how political power works and the extent to which it is controlled by a few select individuals (SeaSrgeant, 2022). The Prime Minister of the UK has, arguably, more power within the political system of his or her country than that of any other Prime Minister in comparable liberal democracies (Seldon et al., 2021). During the Covid crisis, parliament passed new legislation giving the state increased powers in regulating the lives of its citizens in order to enforce the social distancing which was seen as essential for combatting the pandemic. The government also had extensive existing powers to enforce such regulations – all of which, as the anti-lockdown demonstrators correctly noted, restricted many of the normal, everyday freedoms citizens could enjoy under non-emergency circumstances. As Baldwin (2021, p. 12) writes

> The nuts and bolts of democracy are little conducive to swift or incisive decision-making: consensus, checks and balances, due process, and voting. In emergencies, democratic procedures must paradoxically be temporarily sidestepped in order to preserve democracy.

What is noticeable from responses to the Covid pandemic around the world is that the political approach of all administrations has been primarily Hobbesian. That is to say, they have embraced the idea of a system in which power and authority is invested by the people in the state on the understanding that this is the best means of providing protection for them from harm. This was explicitly commented upon by some of the media in the early months of the pandemic (Oliver, 2020), when questions were being raised as to whether authoritarian or semi-authoritarian states were better set up to confront the pandemic because of the culture of state control they possessed (Alon et al., 2020). In effect, however, even liberal democracies operated for the most part in a partially Hobbesian fashion, with the announcement and imposition of laws restricting action.

Despite all this, in a liberal democracy, simply enforcing blanket restrictions is not considered an attractive option. The populace also needed to be persuaded that whatever actions were being taken were the correct actions, and that they were fully justified (Brettschneider, 2010). As the anti-lockdown demonstrations illustrate, the perception that the government is taking unjustified action to coerce the behaviour of citizens is likely to lead to non-cooperation and accusations of tyranny.

Persuasion, in this context, is the act of influencing people's thoughts, feelings and beliefs in order to influence their actions. And there are three main reasons why persuasion was important in this case. The first is that the very idea of liberal democracy is based on the belief that politicians are governing with the consent of the people. This consent can, in theory, be withdrawn at any time, and various practices and systems have evolved over centuries in order to protect against the overreach of the leader. The most notable of these is the occurrence of regular elections where a party needs to be able to persuade the electorate to continue to grant their consent. Secondly, and very much linked to this, is that the politician's career and reputation rely on keeping on the right side of public opinion, and they will not wish to sacrifice this if at all possible. As one of the few codified explanations of the role of Prime Minister, *The Cabinet Manual* (Cabinet Office, 2011, p. 21), explains:

> The Prime Minister is the head of the Government and holds that position by virtue of his or her ability to command the confidence of the House of Commons, which in turn commands the confidence of the electorate, as expressed through a general election. The Prime Minister's unique position of authority also comes from support in the House of Commons.

Finally there is the need for people to follow the regulations – something which is achieved far more easily if they do so of their own volition rather than simply out of fear of punishment (Pennings and Symons, 2021). The Hobbesian pact may provide the infrastructure for the politics of crisis management, but it needs to be wrapped in the rhetoric of consensus politics.

Within this context then, what is it that counts as good leadership in times of crisis? And what can an examination of this question tell us about both political persuasion and the current nature of British politics?

The subject of this book is mediated leadership within a political system which relies primarily on consensual adherence to restrictions rather than coerced adherence. Within this system a hugely important part of leadership is communicating a clear plan of action and persuading the populace to follow it. It matters, of course, whether the plan of action is effective and the extent to which it is managed and executed in a successful way. Good leadership also entails overseeing this latter point (the management and execution) and working with scientists and public health officials to formulate the former (an effective plan of action). But in a liberal democracy such as the UK, the communication and persuasion elements of leadership are as important as anything else, and thus worth detailed analysis.

The way that any mediated communication operates is determined by a number of context-specific factors. Firstly, there is the nature of the political system in which everything is taking place. There will be conventions, customs and constraints which shape the way that government communications are carried out. As Baldwin (2021, pp. 9–10) puts it, 'How we seek to spare ourselves the ravages of pandemics reflects the assumptions baked into our political culture and the systems that govern us.' Secondly, there is the media landscape that exists across the country, which involves both the relationship between press and politicians, the disparate aims of the news media and the consumer habits of the audience. It is within a context influenced by these factors that any leadership takes place.

Another crucial factor is the character of the leader and the way this is presented by the media. Issues of character – especially in terms of 'charisma' – have been central to theories of leadership, as will be discussed later. Boris Johnson offers a fascinating case study in this regard, given his status as a celebrity politician (Wood et al., 2016). And a great part of the public picture of his celebrity character is related to his style of communication.

Johnson himself has invested heavily in the idea of a systemised approach to public relations as a vital part of modern politics: from hiring a press secretary along the model of the Whitehouse to plans for converting a room in 10 Downing Street into a dedicated Press Briefing Centre (Landler, 2020). Yet for all this, the image of his premiership is less to do with smoothly executed spin and more with reliance on a somewhat shambolic charisma. Here too, however, a focus on communication is central. In 2019, when running for the leadership of the Conservative Party, Johnson made a defence of his style of communication in terms which would be very familiar to other populist leaders (Block and Negrine, 2017):

> One of the reasons that the public feels alienated now from us [politicians] as a breed, is because too often they feel that we are muffling and veiling our language, not speaking as we find – covering everything up in bureau-cratic platitudes, when what they want to hear is what we genuinely think. If sometimes in the cause of trying to get across what I genuinely think, I use phrases and language that have caused offence, of course I am sorry for the offence I have caused, but I will continue to speak as directly as I can. (Quoted in Woodcock, 2019)

The style in which he expresses himself, he argues, is a mark of authenticity (Luebke, 2021), which in turn can be read as a desire to be honest with the British public. In a statement such as this, then, there is a metalinguistic argu-ment being made about the how style indexes character, which situates com-munication at the heart of the business of leadership.

Then, of course, there's the other side of the coin. In the spring of 2021, some months after he'd left his job as special advisor to the Prime Minister, Dominic Cummings wrote of Johnson that:

> He rewrites reality in his mind afresh according to the moment's demands. He lies – so blatantly, so naturally, so regularly – that there is no real distinction possible with him, as there is with normal people, between truth and lies. He always tells people what they want to hear and he never means it. He always says 'I can't remember' when they remind him and is rarely 'lying'. (Cummings, 2021)

Here again the argument is that the then PM's approach to communication is indexical of his character and, by extension, his suitability for the role. Although in Cummings's case his interpretation of what is being indexed is very different from Johnson's. Many of the views in this quote are ones which had been levelled at Johnson by the media throughout his career as both journalist and politician (Collins, 2021). But it is perhaps notable that they were made in this instance by someone who had been seen, only a few months earlier, as the *éminence grise* behind Johnson's premiership. One year on and the same allegations were again being made in the *Mirror* article cited above, yet Johnson was still holding on to power. And it is here perhaps that it is worth remembering that despite media focus on the personality-based nature of leadership, procedural issues to do with the legal-rational system which consti-tutes a country's political workings are equally vital. It is often bureaucracy rather than charisma which determines how a scenario plays out.

Overview of the Book

In order to lay the foundations for an analysis of the ways in which the government's communications strategy suffered a perceived loss of trust and authority as the social situation caused by the pandemic unfolded, the book will start by looking at the relationship between leadership and communication in politics, and the roles that the concepts of trust and authority play in this. It will do this through an analysis of how the daily government briefings on the Covid situation were arranged as a genre of public communication, as well as of key events which were perceived, by the media, as undermining or contradicting the messaging, and which led to accusations of hypocrisy in the government's behaviour.

The book focuses on three specific communicative events: the first of the daily Covid briefings which took place on 16 March 2020; the impromptu press briefing given by the Prime Minister's special advisor Dominic Cummings on 25 May 2020, after it was reported in the press that he had allegedly broken lockdown by travelling from London to Durham (in the north of England) at the end of March that year; and Cummings's subsequent appearance before the joint Health and Social Care Committee and Science and Technology Committee into 'Lessons Learnt' almost exactly a year after his impromptu press briefing. The analysis focuses on the ways the government indexed authority and trustworthiness as part of their communications strategy in terms not simply of the verbal discourse used during the press briefings, but also the configuration and deployment of other semiotic resources which, when combined in a particular formulation, created an emergent genre of political communication in the shape of the Covid briefings. In contrast, the Dominic Cummings press briefing did not conform to this particular genre, nor indeed to any other established genre (at least in respect of its details), but was instead an ad hoc communicative event, hastily arranged and executed in response to what was seen at the time as a growing public relations crisis. Again, however, issues relating to trust and authority were invoked, both in the verbal discourse and in elements of presentation. The third event – Cummings's appearance before the select committee – then provided a very different narrative on events from the earlier press briefing, and included an account of the aims and rationale for how the initial explanation fitted within the government's communication strategy at the time.

The choice of these three events as the focus of the analysis is motivated by the fact that the first was an officially established tool for leadership, while the second was ad hoc and responsive, and thus taken together the first two provide a picture of the scope and limitations of the communicative strategy employed by the government. The third event provides reflective testimony on this strategy by one of the participants a year later, by which time the political situation had changed significantly. It thus aims to supplement the analysis of the ad hoc press conference by what later account says of how the earlier account was designed as a piece of persuasion, as well as looking at how the later event was structured as a piece of persuasion in its own right.

It is perhaps worth stressing that the political ramifications of decisions and actions taken with respect to the handling of the Covid crises did not, in any sense, end with the third event examined in the book. A little over a year after Cummings's appearance before the select committee, Boris Johnson was forced to resign as Prime Minister, in great part due to the loss of trust following a string of perceived breaches of his government's Covid regulations. Even now at time of writing, two Prime Ministers later, similar issues are headline news again ('Matt Hancock told breaking Covid rules was "slap in face"') as the former Health Secretary features in a reality TV programme (McIntosh, 2022).

The methodology employed by the book involves discursively reconstructing in some detail the ways in which these communicative acts were arranged and carried out, with a particular focus on the indexical factors which constituted the context in which the meaning of each event and its messaging was interpreted. Particular focus is given to the way meaning was shaped by the broader chronotopic contexts (i.e., those relating to time and place) in which the government's communications were circulated, interpreted and debated; and how subsequent events created counter-narratives which ultimately destabilised communications over the pandemic. This approach involves a necessarily eclectic mix of analytic tools, including discourse analysis, multimodal analysis and narrative analysis, focusing predominantly on video and transcript data of the three chosen events, along with instances from the news media of how reaction to events was framed. As will be illustrated, a focus on chronology played a vital role in the interpretation of the official narratives (see, for example, newspaper articles offering a chronology of Cummings's actions [e.g., ITV, 2020b]), and for this reason a key analytic concept I draw on here is the idea of the chronotope as a structuring device for the understanding of context (De Fina, 2019). By examining the ways in which the messaging was framed by the government and re-framed by the media and public, the book thus explores the ways in which political leadership operates as mediated discourse in modern society.

2 Conceptualising Leadership

Typologies of Leadership

Before moving to the communicative events themselves, it is worth firstly considering how 'leadership' is conceptualised in a context of this sort, and the role played by the key indexicals of trust and authority within leadership discourse in politics. 'Leadership' is a much-overused term in various sectors of society these days, with its popularity resulting in criticism that it is often employed as little more than a buzzword with very little actual substance attached (see, for example, the critiques of vagueness associated with its use in the education sector in Torrance and Humes [2015]). As a pivotal symbol in the management discourses of various sectors, the term, along with similar buzzwords (Mautner, 2005), has a specific profile to its meaning depending on the discursive context in which it is used. For this reason, its use as an analytic concept needs to be interpreted within the specific discursive context in which it is being employed. In the context of higher education, for example, leadership is used to denote a particular form of managerial conduct which is required for promotion and is measured according to criteria informed by a standard set of neoliberal attitudes (Amsler and Shore, 2017). Leadership in contemporary higher education is thus very different from, say, the type of leadership demonstrated by the commander of a platoon of soldiers, or even the captain of a football team.

As the example from higher education suggests, there is always an evaluative element to the concept, and any discussion about political leadership in contexts such as this is in essence going to be a discussion about 'effective' leadership. It is not merely a description of the visible actions and apparent decisions of the person who is occupying a leadership role but will instead also involve a focus on the effects of these actions and decisions. Any theory of political leadership includes an idea of the expectations that a community can have for what their leader can offer them, and in many theories of leadership it is these expectations which provide the justification for people granting executive power to the leader.

It is, of course, very difficult to determine what counts as effective leadership in complex contexts such as a pandemic, when the variables which shape the overall situation are both multifarious and ongoing. In cases such as the example from higher education, effectiveness is determined by various institutional criteria; that is, the label of leadership is bestowed on someone (either on their actions or simply on their role, as per Grint's four definitional approaches to leadership below) as a result of their being adjudged to fulfil these criteria. In the case of the government, this evaluation process includes procedures such as elections, votes of no confidence, along with media opinion (and, to an extent, public opinion, although this is usually mediated by the news media), all of which act to either sustain or rescind leadership status. It is for this reason that it is important to consider any acts of leadership within the specific contexts in which they take place and in light of the criteria used to evaluate them.

What does this then mean with respect to the UK government's leadership in the context of the Covid pandemic, and the sense expressed in the news media that this was found wanting at certain stages?

To understand why media opinion began to criticise the government's actions, one first needs to determine what, in a context of this sort, qualifies as adequate or successful leadership. It is worth beginning, perhaps, by sketching out a schema for conceptualising leadership, and for this we can start with Dahl's (1957) influential idea that power can best be defined as the ability to get someone to do something they would not otherwise do, and append to this the idea that leadership is the nature of that ability. Leadership is, of course, somewhat broader than this, as it can also involve inspiring or coordinating group action in circumstances where there is no reluctance on the part of the population. But for the context of leadership in times of pandemic, when restrictions on behaviour are felt to be necessary for the greater good, the above definition can be a useful starting point.

Grint (2005), synthesising the extensive literature on the topic, identifies four different approaches to leadership. There is:

- Leadership as position
- Leadership as person
- Leadership as result
- Leadership as process

The first of these refers to the way that leadership is a characteristic bestowed upon a person based on their position within an organisation or community. By virtue of being the Head of Department, for instance, the person given this role is deemed to have a leadership position. This usually involves being at the head of a vertical hierarchy of some sort, be it institutional or societal more generally. With this position come a number of tools of coercion which the leader has available to them to assist with executing various tasks.

An alternative model, particularly popular in the discourse of politics, is leadership based upon the personality, image or behaviour of the leader. This is often related to the idea of the 'born leader', whereby inherent character traits mean that some people are supposedly able to attract and influence followers on the strength of their personality alone, while others are not (Avolio, 2004).

One of the most influential theorists of political leadership, even a century after his death, is Max Weber (1947 [1922]), with his concept of charismatic leadership. In the schema he developed, this was contrasted with the notion of legal, rational authority; the latter consisting of authority established through law, rationality-based norms and a system of bureaucracy, while the former is founded on the outstanding qualities and enigmatic power of the leader's character. This idea has continued to prove its relevance in recent years with the rise of populist leaders, and the ways in which their appeal and authority is constructed. Despite the bureaucratic political system that operates in the UK, the idea of a charismatic leader is still intensely important in media coverage of political activity.

The third approach in Grint's taxonomy – and the most obviously evaluative of the four – is leadership as a matter of getting things done, i.e., a good or effective leader is one who achieves significant outcomes. Falling within this category is what James (2015a, 2015b) refers to as the statecraft model, based on what he calls 'cunning leadership', which has as its aim the winning of elections, a competence in governance, and the maintaining of power. There are five elements to this: a winning electoral strategy; the cultivation of a reputation for competent governing, especially as regards economic affairs; the successful management of the political party; the ability to gain dominance in the battle of ideas; and the successful management of the constitution in terms of taking advantage of electoral laws, voting regulations and so forth. In this model, the 'things that get done' are primarily finding ways to take and keep hold of power. Liz Truss's brief premiership in the autumn of 2022 is a striking example of the way that adverse outcomes can quickly undermine a leader's status.

As a complement – or perhaps contrast – to 'leadership as result' is the fourth category, which focuses on *how* it is that leaders get things done, and views this as the most important factor for defining the concept of leadership. This is often embodied in the idea of the exemplary leader – one whose own conduct and actions provide a model of good, and perhaps inspirational, behaviour for their followers.

Whichever approach one favours, any discussion of political leadership needs to take into account the political system in which such leadership occurs and be sensitive to the dynamics and constraints of that system for the way that decisions are made and communicated, and the causal relations between such decision-making and action. In other words, there are important questions of political philosophy which provide the context for any analyses of notions of 'leadership' in instances such as this. As Benjamin Constant said, in one of the earliest tracts in the development of the liberal tradition, it is not so much a question of who has the authority but of how that authority is managed (2003 [1815]).

A point worth making, therefore, is that the actions of the leadership – and specifically particular leaders – may well be far less influential than media representations of and comments about events make out. There tends to be a hyperbolic dramatisation of events in the interpretation given within the media in its desire to favour narratives centred around individuals and their personal struggles (Seargeant, 2020, 2023), and this likely assigns more power and influence to particular politicians and public figures than is fully justified.

Forms of Compliance

A companion to Grint's taxonomy is Etzioni's (1964) categorisation of different forms of compliance, which also has a bearing on the type of leadership best suited to a crisis like Covid, and introduces the topic of communication into the equation. Etzioni distinguishes between three different types of power which can secure compliance:

* Coercive power
* Remunerative or utilitarian power
* Normative power

The first of these is that which exists in institutions such as the army or prisons: you do what I say or you face repercussions. In a political context this is the law-based system which underpins social organisation. Secondly there is remunerative power, which is based on being rewarded (e.g., through a salary) for compliance. Finally, there is normative compliance which is based around shared values and other forms of symbolic affiliation.

These different categories map broadly onto the different types of problems which leadership is often forced to address. If the problem is a crisis of some sort, it likely calls for coercive compliance. More everyday problems – those which a managerial approach can deal with – can get by with remunerative compliance. While more complex problems – those which are long-term – call for normative compliance, as people need to commit to helping on the basis of shared beliefs and values (i.e., this is a predominantly cultural rather than legal framework for compliance). Covid has been framed, from the beginning, as a crisis and thus, as we have seen, involves coercive regulations in the shape of new laws. Yet, as noted, this approach is ideologically in conflict with many of the shared values – or at least the idea of these values – which constitute national identity in the UK (and other Western societies), and thus coercive compliance alone is not enough. Which brings us to the need for persuasion.

Leadership, Communication and 'Voice'

The importance of the relationship between leadership and communication has been highlighted in several studies. For example, Hackman and Johnson (2013, p. 11) place communication at the heart of their definition of leadership, which they describe as a 'human (symbolic) communication that modifies the attitudes and behaviors of others in order to meet shared group goals and needs' (see also Fetzer and Bull, 2012; Clifton et al., 2019; and Neustadt, 1991, on the idea that the US presidency is founded on the power to persuade). Similar assertions have been made by several politicians themselves over the years (Seargeant, 2020). For instance, in an interview with the journalist Tom McTague (2021) Boris Johnson argued that 'People live by narrative . . . Human beings are creatures of the imagination', and that the role of the leader is thus to craft a story that resonates with the electorate.

This importance of persuasive communication is clearly exemplified in the way that the briefings and press conferences held by the government during the Covid pandemic had a dual purpose. On the one hand they acted as key sources of information about the pandemic and its implications for the local context, including the introduction of specific regulative measures. But they also, importantly, operated as a platform for urging the public to commit to doing their own part to aid the response; that is, to willingly submit to the compliance measures without the need for the threat of penalties. This involved the modifying of attitudes and behaviours via persuasion.

If we adopt a value-neutral approach to the concept of propaganda (Lasswell, 1928) – that is, the idea that propaganda is not solely the insidious manipulation of opinion via deception but is about shaping people's beliefs and attitudes either for positive or negative purposes – then these campaigns of persuasion operate along propagandistic lines in that they are designed to intentionally influence the thinking and behaviour of the public towards the government's agenda. They are not necessarily deceitful or excessively manipulative in terms of method (deceit and manipulation being features of the popular modern understanding of propaganda), but they rely nonetheless on planned and coordinated strategies of persuasion designed for a specific purpose (what Ellul [1973] refers to as vertical propaganda).

A basic model of the considerations needed for effective propaganda is given in Figure 1. The communication is goal-oriented in that it has some aim or outcome in mind. It is targeted at a particular audience, and its message and style is shaped accordingly. In so far as the communication is a prompt to action it needs to factor in the practicalities that facilitate that action and ensure its aims are consistent with these practicalities. And finally, it follows a certain set of tenets in terms of the practices it adopts.

There is one further important concept to consider: the sociolinguistic notion of 'voice'. This refers to the ability, when communicating, not merely to articulate an utterance, but to have that utterance be heard and understood by others (Hymes, 1996). To persuade someone, one needs to mobilise the semiotic

What is the
Purpose ?

The overarching purpose is to influence people's opinions and beliefs, sometimes with the aim of manipulating their actions

This can be focused on

- something specific (e.g. voting)
- people's worldview more generally
- or it can simply be a way to undermine current beliefs

The actions it motivates can be

- to provide support for an objective (e.g. win a election)
- to create antipathy towards an idea or group
- to create scepticism and dissent, in order to destabilise or impair the current situation

Who are the
Audience ?

Any act of propaganda needs to target a specific audience and take account of the nature of that audience

The propaganda should be shaped according to the audience's

- ability to effect change
- relevant or useful beliefs they already have (whereby the aim may be more to reinforce rather than change these)
- their pressure points for provoking an emotional reaction

What is the underlying
System ?

What are mechanisms of power that exist in the culture and determine how change takes place?

- the ways in which power is distributed
- the nature of the media environment and its influence on politics
- the mechanism by which voting or other forms of influence happens
- the schedule of the political system (e.g. timings of elections)

What is the
Process ?

The core element of any process of propaganda is the appeal to emotion and identity

The key emotions here are HOPE and FEAR

In identity terms the appeal is to a sense of belonging and a sense of pride in the community and its culture

Figure 1 The four steps to effective propaganda

resources one has to hand in such a way as to get one's message across (Blommaert, 2005).

There are two aspects to this. Firstly, there is voice as production; that is, the way one creates a message with whatever resources one has available, for the purposes of effective communication. Secondly, there is voice as uptake; that is to say, the social dynamics which lead to people taking note of what one says. For successful uptake, the speaker needs to index contextual factors which satisfy certain evaluative expectations of the audience as these expectations represent general embedded beliefs about social acts of communication. Or to put it another way, an utterance points not only to the referential meaning (that encoded in the syntax and semantics of the utterance), but also a social meaning which is interpreted by the hearers within the broader social context in which it is made (Agha, 2007). Verbal communication always indexes a great deal about the social context of the speaker and their relationship with the audience, and this – along with other elements of the physical and mediated environment – forms the context in which the utterance is made meaningful and provides it with pragmatic force. Or to put it another way, voice is also something which can be enhanced through the curation of the context in which an utterance is made.

Leadership, by its very definition, requires a sense of authority over an audience so that the leader's opinions and directions are heeded (Partington, 2018). Likewise, the force of a message is reliant on the audience trusting what the speaker says sufficiently enough to feel compelled to act on any directives (McMyler, 2011). In liberal democracies especially, where authority is reliant in part on public support, trust is a key element in this equation (Warren, 2018). As such, the indexing of both authority and trust is vital in the production of voice for government communication (this is equally true of contexts such as journalism, as demonstrated in Siltaoja [2009] and Vos and Thomas [2018]). To understand how this was achieved (or at least, attempted) in the case of the UK government's response to the Covid crisis, we need to examine the way the context for communication of the messaging was constructed and managed.

Media–Source Relations

The wider context for any political communication is media–source relations, that is, the often significant influence that the relationship between journalists and politicians (and their advisors) can have on the way the news is shaped (Johnston, 2020). In today's Westminster politics, this relationship is very much institutionalised: journalists from prominent media outlets have access both to spaces and to personnel within the government and often rely on their connections with politicians and their advisors for some of the information which becomes the news. Likewise, politicians use this relationship as a means of attempting to circulate their own message, either officially or unofficially. The tradition of the 'anonymous high-ranking source' or the strategic leak falls into this latter category, whereby someone in the government is able to feed a story into the media cycle by means of the relationship they have with a sympathetic journalist. Despite the often adversarial nature of the relationship between press and politician, both sides see advantages for themselves in ensuring that this relationship is maintained.

The use of broadcast media for prime-ministerial communications is a relatively recent development, however fundamental it might now be to the job. The 'mediafication' of the role of Prime Minister did not properly begin until 1924, when Stanley Baldwin made use of a radio broadcast as part of his campaigning in that year's general election (Hennessy, 1998). Ramsay MacDonald was the first Prime Minister to appoint a 'press secretary', in 1931, and by the end of that decade, in 1938, broadcasting equipment was first installed in Number 10 (Seldon et al., 2021). Just over a year later Neville Chamberlain used this to announce that Britain was at war with Germany. As has been noted, Boris Johnson made a number of moves to further expand the paraphernalia for press access at Downing Street.

While the dynamics of media–source relationship plays a part in shaping news representation of politics, there is also much meta-discussion of the ethics, legitimacy and import of aspects of this relationship (Esser and Strömbäck, 2014). The media, in the opinion of many, should maintain a marked independence from the government as a way of preserving their objectivity. To do otherwise risks them becoming little more than a propaganda outlet for government policy. Naïve versions of this view – that is, ones which take little account of the practicalities involved in modern media–source relations – are very common on social media. The BBC, for example, is regularly attacked for pro-government bias based on the perceived relationship that some of its journalists have with prominent politicians (Mills, 2016). Notwithstanding this, modern political leadership involves constant management of the media–source relationship given the fundamental role it plays in the communications process.

Media–source relations are conventionally approached from the perspective of the structural factors which facilitate such relations and how these are used for circulating information. From a discursive point of view, information travels from person to person and context to context, and in doing so is invariably both recontextualised and reframed in the process of being broadcast to the public. Of note for all the three events I am looking at in this book is that they all act as institutionalised and authorised forums for media–source relations (as opposed to, for example, the unsanctioned leak), and all lead to the co-creation of information which is a product of these practices of recontextualisation and reframing – that's to say, they provide discursive content from politicians which is then repackaged by the media in the form of television bulletins and newspaper articles. But they also act as means of broadcasting information directly to audiences who watch the live or recorded stream of them, and thus provide a mostly 'unprocessed' version of the politicians' discourse.

3 The Government Press Briefing

The Performance of Institutional Authority in Political Contexts

British politics prior to the Covid crisis had been dominated by the UK's withdrawal from the European Union. A general election held in December 2019 was viewed in many parts of the media as a referendum on the two major parties' approaches to Brexit (e.g., Kettle, 2019), with the Conservatives, led by Boris Johnson, winning a sizeable majority with their simple pledge to 'Get Brexit Done', versus Jeremy Corbyn's Labour Party's far less transparent proposals. In January 2020, the Withdrawal Bill that had been negotiated by Johnson's government passed through parliament, and on 31 January the UK officially left the EU and moved into the one-year transition period. For the government and its supporters this was cause for much celebration, not least because it appeared to deliver on Johnson's promises during the election, in contrast to the two earlier pledges by Conservative governments which had to be broken when the Prime Minster at the time (Theresa May in the first instance, Johnson in the second) was forced to ask for a delay to the withdrawal date.

It has been argued that the intense focus on Brexit around this time meant that the government was slow to respond to the seriousness of the early spread of Covid (e.g., Hopkin, 2020). Italy, as the first major hotspot in Europe, went into full lockdown on 9 March 2020, after a number of weeks of more localised measures to combat the disease. Back in the UK at this time there was little decisive action being taken, but a great deal of squabbling going on. Politicians and the media were embroiled in a debate about 'herd immunity', following ambiguous remarks made by Johnson in a television interview (Krishna, 2020). There was also much comment in the news media about the way that Johnson appeared to dismiss the severity of the situation (e.g., Calvert et al., 2020), and take a generally complacent approach to the need to respond to it (Sanders, 2020). For instance, he boasted about shaking hands with hospital staff on the same day that his government's Scientific Advisory Group for Emergencies (Sage) were warning against physical contact of this sort (Mason, 2020); and it was later revealed that he had failed to personally attend the first five meetings of COBRA (Cabinet Office Briefing Rooms committee), the government's emergency committee, at which Covid was discussed (Walker, 2020). Lockdown for the country was not announced until 23 March 2020, and only came into effect on 26 March, by which time it was estimated that 1.5 million people in the UK had already been infected (Finnis, 2020). One of the aims of the Covid briefings when they were introduced in March, therefore, was to present an image of control over the situation, of visible leadership and of general public reassurance, following this period of media criticism.

There are two very important issues of timing related to the leadership status of Boris Johnson throughout the Covid crisis. The first is that he had, as noted, just convincingly won a general election and thus, in terms of the political cycle, the party he was leading was at the very beginning of a five-year term in government. Opportunities within the regular workings of the system for the public to pass judgement on his leadership would not occur again for several years. (This was in notable contrast to Donald Trump's position in the United States in 2020, where the pandemic coincided with an election year.)

The second issue of timing was the passing of the bill effecting the UK's exit from the European Union which brought to a close months of political struggle about the content of the withdrawal bill. The promise to see this through was the central plank of the Conservatives' general election campaign, and Johnson had positioned himself in the months leading up to the election as the one person able to do this. This positioning involved casting himself as an anti-establishment figure, taking an antagonistic approach to institutional authority and using a variety of populist tropes to communicate this. In the six months leading up to the outbreak of the pandemic, the relationship between the bureaucratic, rule-based system and Johnson's style of charismatic leadership had produced a number of flash points. Each of these ended up reaffirming the authority of the system as it traditionally operated, but at the same time they bolstered a discourse of the populist leader fighting on behalf of the people against this stifling system. These incidents saw the government attempting to push decisions through the political process without adequately consulting parliament, most noticeably when Johnson attempted to prorogue parliament in 2019. In this case, a legal challenge was brought against the government and the courts ruled that the action had been illegal because, according to the president of the supreme court, it 'prevented parliament from carrying out its constitutional role' (quoted in Bowcott et al., 2019). By January 2020, however, Boris Johnson's strategy of taking an antagonistic line towards traditional parliamentary procedures had produced the desired outcome by convincing the electorate to back him overwhelmingly in the general election, thus allowing him to proceed now within the bounds of parliamentary procedure.

Another major factor for the context of the politics of the pandemic in the UK was the rise in what often gets referred to as post-truth politics (Ball, 2017). Second only to Donald Trump, Boris Johnson had emerged as the poster boy for this form of political communication, regularly making statements which were provably false, yet refusing to acknowledge the misleading message he was promulgating even when presented with conclusive counterevidence (Oborne, 2021).

The result was that prior to the Covid crisis there had been an assault from Johnson's leadership both on the traditional institutions of liberal democracy in the UK, and on the values of truth in consequential political communication from the government. Despite this (or perhaps in part because of it), support for Johnson's leadership across the country remained strong, as evidenced by his success in the December 2019 general election, and both practically and reputationally he was in a well-grounded position at the time when the Covid crisis struck.

Briefing the Press

Between the middle of March 2020 when they began, to late June when they were initially abandoned as a regular occurrence, there were 92 daily Covid briefings, along with two national addresses by the Prime Minister (BBC News, 2020). The format for the briefings involved a cabinet minister flanked by scientific and medical experts, standing at podiums in a room in 10 Downing Street, with journalists seated in rows in front of them or later, when face-to-face gatherings were prohibited, appearing on a large monitor at the side of the room. After the first few sessions, Boris Johnson usually only appeared himself when there were major announcements to make. For instance, on Sunday 24 May, he made one of these increasingly rare appearances in order to defend Dominic Cummings following the revelations around alleged breach of lockdown.

The press conference is one particular example of the organisation of media–source relations. It is a publicly facing one, where the details of how this relationship is managed are on display, via the live streaming of the event, to an audience on the internet. Of course, what is broadcast via the live-stream is only part of what takes place. To borrow Goffman's term (1990 [1959]), it is the 'frontstage' element, which has been designed for broadcast. The 'backstage' element in this case will consist of the off-air discussions with politicians and advisors, as well as the organisational communications that manage the staging of the event.

What we have in the presentation of the press conference is predominantly legal-rational authority (in Weberian terms) conveyed through the institutions of the system. Authority is communicated via a complex of contextual features which provide status for the leader's words. For the most part, leadership is a product not of the personality of the individual politician (i.e., of Boris Johnson as himself), but of the office being represented. For this to apply, the politician needs to conform to the expectations of the occasion in terms of behaviours, rather than violate these expectations. Of interest in this particular scenario is the way that Boris Johnson is primarily viewed as a leader whose popularity (which led to his election as leader) is based on his personality. His authority within his own party, at least in the aftermath of the general election, was in great part a product of the idea that his image had helped bring about the win. But the communicative dynamics of the press conference downplayed the idea of charisma as leadership, and instead stressed institutional authority.

A notable contrast here was between Covid press conferences held by Johnson and those by Donald Trump when he was US President. Trump is likewise seen as a leader whose personality connects with the electorate (or at least, enough of the electorate for him to win the 2016 presidential election). The style of leadership that he had built around this personality was on display in the press conferences he gave, as it was in nearly all his public performances. Trump was far more unpredictable, often not conforming to the expected style or behaviour of the occasion, but instead improvising in his comments in ways which disturbed his colleagues. This often created a sense of conflict with his team (particularly the medical professionals) which destabilised the coherence of an approach based on institutional authority. As far as the Covid press conferences went, this aspect of Johnson's persona was not to the fore as it often was in other contexts.

Chronotopes as Context

To examine in more detail the way the press conferences worked as communicative events in this context, it will be useful to view them from the point of view of the chronotope. The concept of the chronotope, derived from the writings on literary studies of Mikhail Bakhtin (1981) and then adapted for various analytic purposes within sociolinguistics (see De Fina [2019] and Kroon and Swanenberg [2019] for overviews of some of these) has been both highly influential and, arguably, somewhat over-extended, in its use. The principal insight it provides for any understanding of the way that meaning is generated in discourse is that context is a result of factors related to the combination of both time and space (Blommaert and De Fina, 2017).

Different genres of communication are often a result of the expectations related to a particular chronotope – that is, a particular confluence of time-specific and space-/place-specific conventions which provide the parameters in which acts of communication are to be understood; or, as Blommaert and De Fina (2017, p. 3) express it, 'chronotopes invoke orders of indexicality valid in a specific timespace frame … [which] enable, allow, and sanction specific modes of behavior as positive, desired, or compulsory … and this happens through the deployment and appraisal of chronotopically relevant indexicals'. A chronotope can be seen as complex of conventions or beliefs related to a specific time and place, which contribute to, and shape, a genre of communication (Crossley, 2007). If we take as an example a consultation with the doctor, this takes place at a pre-determined time (that of the appointment) and in a specific location (the doctor's surgery); the roles imposed by the genre of the consultation are doctor and patient, and there are a set of modes of interaction (doctor-led questioning), as well as the use of particular discourses (a medical register, which is often then glossed or 'translated' into what is deemed appropriate for a lay audience) which govern the encounter. The authority of the doctor as expert is indexed by several of these elements (e.g., the use of medical discourse) which together create the chronotope.

The practices which constitute a communicative genre of this sort are both conventional and a mixture of the explicit and the implicit. Due to this latter point it is often when traditions or beliefs about these conventions are violated in specific communicative events that we are best able to trace their outlines. In the context of political leadership, there have been a number of recent examples of chronotopic conventions in US politics being violated and leading to controversy over the significance that such violation can have for the potential impact of the communicative event. During the 2020 Republican National Convention (RNC), for instance, when Donald Trump was accepting his party's nomination for the November presidential election, both he and members of his team were criticised for exploiting government symbols for partisan electoral purposes. Trump himself broke with convention and delivered his acceptance speech from the White House, thus violating the prohibition on using government property (and the symbolic and indexical value attached to it) for what was a party, rather than national, matter. Likewise, Secretary of State Mike Pompeo addressed the online RNC while on an official diplomatic visit to Jerusalem, and in doing so violated two established conventions: the expectation that Secretaries of State do not participate in partisan electoral politics, and that they do not use the trappings of their office for partisan electoral purposes (Lawson, 2020).

In both cases, controversy arose not from what was said in their respective speeches, but from the context in which these were delivered, and the particular form of authority these contexts indexed and thus, potentially, bestowed on the speakers and their speeches in light of the conventions for such speeches (i.e., the enhancement of voice). Conventions dictating the expected conduct of serving officials stumping for their individual parties prohibit the use of government institutions, and to flout these is to be in danger of violating the Hatch Act, a law introduced in the 1930s to prevent federal employees from engaging in explicit partisan political activity while acting in an official capacity. With respect to Trump's use of the White House for his acceptance speech, the U.S. Office of Special Counsel subsequently ruled that he was not, in fact, in violation of this law (Hamrick, 2020; Quinn, 2020), but nonetheless it was seen in many quarters as a flagrant flouting of convention (Mazza, 2020). For instance, Walter Shaub (2020), the former White House ethics chief, wrote that 'This abomination may be the most visible misuse of official position for private gain in America's history. It is an abuse of the power entrusted to this man, the breach of a sacred trust'. Situation-specific discourse conventions, in a context such as this, are thus seen as highly significant.

If we take the example of UK government Covid briefings, we find a very specific set of time-, place- and personnel-related features, all of which were newly combined in this formation for the particular situation (i.e., for briefing the press on daily news about the Covid situation and the government's response), but which drew for precedent on similar scenarios (generic government briefings), as well as the professional roles and identities of those involved. These particular briefings thus had a particular format, which included everything from the material context (a room within in an institutional setting, which was laid out in a particular configuration), the personnel and their physical positioning within this.

In terms of acts of persuasion, the briefings followed the pattern laid out in the four dimensions of the model for propaganda introduced in the previous section. The *purpose* behind the persuasion in this case was a specific one. It was meant to encourage people to abide by the advice and new legal regulations the government was introducing. A secondary purpose may have been to cast the government in a good light and convince the public that they were conscientiously doing their job. This, after all, is a background consideration for all politicians in election-based systems.

The *audience* for the communication was UK residents. The briefings were broadcast live, so to some extent the politicians were addressing the public directly. Those present or able to ask questions however were representatives from the news media (until the occasional question was later included from members of the public). The media then had the ability to amplify and frame the message, while it was the members of the public who needed to take action in their everyday lives on the basis of this message.

The *system*, as we have discussed above, is one in which compliance is generally sought by means of a mixture of all three of Etzioni's (1964) categories: the coercive, the remunerative and the normative. In this case, new legal regulations were being imposed, along with the threat of penalties such as fines for violating these. But the coercive approach was accompanied for both practical and ideological reasons by persuasion campaigns. On the practical side, voluntary compliance is far more effective and frictionless than mechanisms of enforcement. On the ideological side, a tradition of liberal values which underpins the national political consciousness means that public and press alike will be quick to criticise anything which too closely resembles an authoritarian approach.

Finally, the *process* involved appeals to both emotion and identity. The key emotion here was fear, though not of the manufactured type that divisive propaganda so often relies on. It was the genuine fear of the effects of the disease, both in terms of its medical symptoms and the social disruption it was causing. In terms of identity, a great deal was made of the shared commitment to the ideals represented by the NHS, along with the communities which staffed it and the other essential services (the concept of 'key workers').

In each category then the press briefings conformed to the principles of this model of persuasion. Effectiveness of the persuasion is not solely to do with identifying the relevant features for any given context however, but also on how the strategy is executed. And it is in this regard that the details of the format and context of performance become important.

The briefings tended towards a set pattern. A panel of members of parliament and experts would firstly show a short presentation on issues such as hospital admissions, deaths and planned initiatives, followed by a question-and-answer session with the media and, from the end of April, the occasional question submitted by members of the public (Waterson et al., 2020). There were certain expectations around the type of outlet which was invited to take part in the questions. For instance, there was some surprised comment on social media when Simon Binns, editor of *LADbible* (a popular publication not usually viewed as part of the established news media), was called upon to ask a question (Spence, 2020). As was also noted at the time however, the audience that *LADbible* reaches is a young adult one, which is precisely who the government needed to be reaching for announcements about lockdown.

This format thus provided a set protocol for the dissemination and interrogation of information, based on long-established norms within society (the status of various news outlets, the official roles of the participants), with this information then broadcast and disseminated via various platforms. Each briefing was broadcast live on the internet by several news organisations, with the accompanying slides and datasets also published online by the government (Gov.uk, 2020a). The content was also written up by newspaper journalists, broadcast in edited form by news outlets on television and circulated in further truncated form on social media. It was, then, a highly mediated process, relying on both traditional and social media, but one which also had a very concrete physical presence in the briefing events themselves.

The first briefing took place on 16 March, with Boris Johnson hosting, flanked by Professor Chris Whitty, the UK's chief medical adviser, and Sir Patrick Vallance, the UK's chief scientific adviser (transcript at: Gov.uk, 2020b; video at: Channel 4, 2020). The podium at which Johnson stood was positioned before a backdrop of two Union flags, and had on its front the website address for the NHS's coronavirus support page (Figure 2). Later, the podiums would have the slogan the government was using to brand their response to the crisis at the time.

How, then, did this set up provide a meaningful – and authoritative – context for the discourse delivered within it?

Of note firstly is that the chronotope is constituted by the location in which it takes place (the official residence of the Prime Minister, with the added decoration of the Union flags on display), and the various personnel involved appearing in their institutional roles – Boris Johnson is there as Prime Minister, Sir Patrick Vallance as chief scientific adviser and so on – and thus the substance of their speech is afforded the authority which goes with these roles as they have been established within British society over decades. To express it within the vocabulary of 'orders of indexicality' (Silverstein, 2003; Blommaert, 2005), various cues within the interaction – for instance, the use of official titles (e.g., honorifics such

Figure 2 First Downing Street Covid briefing

as 'doctor' or 'sir') when the various personnel are being addressed – index macro discourses related to the running of the state and the organisation and dissemination of scientific knowledge within society, which act as structuring devices for the interaction as a whole. Within this context, the distinction between advice and directives, for instance, is all the more salient given that ministers are representatives of the government, which is devising and enacting policy, and thus directives from them often have the weight of law.

Similarly, there are conventions involved in the interaction between government representatives and the press which symbolise, on a general level, beliefs about the role a free press has in interrogating and holding the government to account – beliefs which act as a key element in the self-identity of liberal democracies (and in this particular case, of the UK as one such liberal democracy). To this end, simply the enacting of an open question-and-answer session with the press indexes a commitment to these values, and when questions from members of the public are then added to the equation, these index an added desire for transparency and direct public engagement on the part of the government. All of this, therefore, is designed to index authority and trust based on institutional roles (both political and scientific) and expectations around the relationship between government and public as this is mediated via the press within the country's political system.

The broader context is also important. The first briefing took place before full lockdown was announced (on 23 March), and the day before the Chancellor, Rishi Sunak, unveiled plans for emergency state support for business (Aspinall, 2022). A few days before the briefing, sports organisations had decided to suspend events, and the Chancellor had announced his first round of emergency support. There was, therefore, still much confusion about the specifics of the government response, as well as continued criticism about the early complacency, and thus the theatre of the briefing can be seen as a first attempt to reimpose a sense of control over proceedings. There was a cautious welcome in the media to this approach (e.g., Freedland, 2020) while the majority of the newspaper front pages took a predominantly straightforward approach to detailing the measures announced in the briefing (ITV, 2020a).

Over time, certain features of the genre of the press conference shifted. Several of these changes were in response to health concerns which necessitated, for example, that journalists stopped attending in person and instead appeared by video link. Alterations motivated by health concerns produced little notable controversy, despite altering the general dynamic. When other elements of the format were changed for non-health-related reasons however, these were often seen as politically motivated, and viewed as modifications meant to undermine certain of the values outlined above.

A notable example of this was when the scientific experts were dropped from the briefings, which led to accusations in the media coverage of a lack of transparency by the government and a desire to manipulate the narrative for political ends (Woodcock, 2020). For instance, the Chief Nursing Officer, Ruth May, was allegedly dropped from one televised briefing as she refused to back the actions of Dominic Cummings over his trip to Durham. The acting Liberal Democrat leader at the time, Sir Ed Davey, was reported as saying that this type of decision amounted to 'dismantling trust' in the government's handling of the pandemic (Syal, 2020). In this case, by altering the context that the government had itself created as a means of communicating values such as trust and transparency, the government effectively undermined its own authority and trustworthiness in the delivery of its messaging.

Linguistic Style

There was, of course, also an arrangement of stylistic decisions in the choice of language Johnson used which indexed symbols and structures of authority and, by extension trust, as important context for his communication (Gov.uk, 2020b). Johnson's introductory address in the first briefing covered the regulative measures that were being planned in restricting social interaction between people, and it also sought to justify the nature of these measures, in terms of both their timing and their scope. Whereas Johnson is often a stylistically creative speaker, particularly in his use of unexpected and ornate metaphors (Charteris-Black, 2019), the language used in this address eschewed his usual rhetorical flourishes in favour of a more restrained style. It did, nevertheless, include a number of persuasive tropes aimed at ensuring compliance amongst the audience.

Firstly, there was the citing of scientific authority, both in general terms – 'everything we do is based scrupulously on the best scientific advice' – and with reference to notable institutional bodies – 'according to SAGE [the Scientific Advisory Group for Emergencies] it looks as though we're now approaching the fast growth part of the upward curve' – which indexed long-standing Enlightenment ideals of truth and knowledge (Pagden, 2013). As noted, he was flanked on either side by leading figures from the medical and scientific professions, and the idea of being 'led by the science' became something of a mantra for the political response to the crisis – an ephemeral political catchphrase, in Gupta's (2022) terminology.

There was also reference to international political bodies, and to the dialogue and cooperation that Johnson was engaged in with other heads of state, which both indexed his own status as a world leader and attempted to position his government as being at the vanguard of the international response: 'Over the last few days, I have been comparing notes and talking to leaders around the world and I can tell you that the UK is now leading a growing global campaign amongst all our friends and allies, whether in the G7, the G20, the UN, the IMF.' For the most part Johnson framed the issues from a collective perspective, using the pronoun 'we' predominantly, indicating in most of these instances that he was addressing the public not in his capacity as an individual but as the representative of a government, and indeed as the leader of a nation (and a nation, he declared, which was playing a leading role in the global response).

There were occasional narrative aspects to the briefing, especially in terms of framing the government's response as a coherent series of actions, linked through causality and decision-making, rather than ad hoc shifts in direction: 'And the right moment, *as we've always said*, is to do it when it is most effective ... '; 'Lastly, it remains true *as we have said in the last few weeks* that risks of transmission of the disease at mass gatherings such as sporting events are relatively low. But ... *we advise against* unnecessary social contact of all kinds' (emphases added). There is a very clear dialogic aspect to these assertions, given the criticism in the press that the government had delayed taking decisive action. Instead, Johnson justified his government's actions by evoking ideologies of national pride and capitalist common sense: 'To keep the economy growing, to make sure ... the UK is also at the front of the effort to back business, to back our economy, to make sure that we get through it.'

Taken in sum, the deployment of these various linguistic and semiotic resources was designed to establish a contextual background for the messaging which created an authoritative, persuasive and trustworthy identity from which to deliver information and advice, and in doing so to offer controlled and stable leadership in place of the perceived lack of this that had occurred in the period before the briefings were set up. Much of the persuasive power intended for the text of the briefing came from non-verbal semiotic means: the employment of symbols, configurations and conventions which indexed forms of institutional authority, which provided the foundations for what was then communicated verbally. A sense of authority was also indexed at points within the verbal discourse of the speech through, but this was only one ingredient in the complete performance. As we have seen with the example of dropping the experts from the briefings, however, when the government's own actions then appeared to violate the expectations they themselves had put in place, confidence in the leadership began to suffer and trust (or the lack of it), as the complement of authority, became a key focus. This was to happen again on a critical scale at the end of May of the same year.

4 The Cummings's Press Conference

Crisis Management

The context against which the briefings were conducted shifted dramatically on 27 March 2020 when it was announced that Boris Johnson had contracted the virus himself, was then admitted to hospital on 5 April and went into intensive care on 6 April. There was much sympathy for him reported in the media at this stage (ITV, 2020c) which, on his release from hospital, was to add a sense of authenticity via personal experience to his communication on the topic. By this time, full lockdown across the UK had come into force, and the government had adopted the slogan 'Stay Home, Protect the NHS, Save Lives'. General media attitudes to the government's response were mostly positive at this point, the *Daily Telegraph* going so far as to pronounce the slogan and the values it conveyed as 'perfect' for the job in hand (Hope and Dixon, 2020).

The next shift in background context occurred at the end of May however, when two newspapers, *The Mirror* and *The Guardian*, reported that the Prime Minister's special advisor, Dominic Cummings, had been spotted breaking lockdown by travelling with his family to Durham, and was subsequently spoken to by the police (Weaver, 2020). In dealing with this particular incident, we need to attend to a number of different time frames which became superimposed on each other to create the public version of events as these were reported in the media. These different time scales are as follows:

1. The incident itself, that is, the series of events privately enacted by Dominic Cummings and his family with his trip to Durham. At the time these took place there was no public disclosure of them, and thus they did not, at this stage, function as resources in the political discourse around Covid.
2. The reporting of certain details from this trip in the two newspapers mentioned above. This in turn had a time-significant element to it in that the story was published across two days, with certain details withheld from the initial report. It also led to the impromptu press conference by Cummings at which he initially attempted to explain his actions.
3. Cummings's evidence before the select committee a year later, in which he gave a modified version of the explanation he had given at his press conference. (This will be dealt with in the next section.)

Dominic Cummings had assumed a somewhat talismanic position within the administration in media/public opinion since Boris Johnson had taken over as Prime Minister, partly due to his role as leading strategist in the Vote Leave organisation at the time of the Brexit referendum and then as one of the architects of the Conservatives' 2019 general election victory. As such he had

a far higher profile than political advisors often have, attracting regular headlines referring to him as, for example, the political 'svengali who has made
himself untouchable in Downing Street' (Tominey, 2020).

According to the news reports in *The Mirror* and *The Guardian* in late May,
during the first lockdown period Cummings had driven 264 miles from his home
in London to a house on the farmland owned by his parents, where he stayed for
the next several days, making the occasional excursion out into the local area.
The reason given for this trip, relayed by the government press office, was that
he wanted to ensure that he and his wife had access to childcare for their four-
year-old son as they were both concerned they had contracted the virus. The first
report from the two newspapers occurred on 22 May. A response was made by
a government spokesperson on 23 May, justifying Cummings's actions by
arguing that 'Owing to his wife being infected with suspected coronavirus
and the high likelihood that he would himself become unwell, it was essential
for Dominic Cummings to ensure his young child could be properly cared for',
and adding, partially incorrectly, that 'At no stage was he or his family spoken to
by the police about this matter, as is being reported' (Devlin, 2020). The
reporters from the two newspapers then released further facts about the event
which problematised this initial explanation from the government.

The timeline in which the crisis unfolded is an important part of the context. It
unfolded over a bank holiday weekend, just a few days after the government had
introduced a change in its Covid policy, replacing the 'Stay Home, Protect the
NHS, Save Lives' slogan with a new three-part directive: 'Stay alert, control the
virus, save lives'. Both the messaging and the way in which this had been rolled
out was much criticised at the time (Hickman, 2020). The accompanying advice
appeared vague and confused, while the rollout involved the government first
releasing the slogan on social media without the full context of the new policy,
then pre-briefing certain journalists but failing to notify leaders in Wales and
Scotland before it was then published in the press. The unofficial channel
utilised here (i.e., the private briefing of select journalists) was considered
inappropriate for an issue of this type (York, 2020).

It was in this already unsettled context that the row over Dominic
Cummings's actions took place. As media pressure continued over the
Saturday and Sunday, and because the Prime Minister was intent on avoiding
having to sack his special advisor, a press conference was hastily arranged for
the purposes of attempting to stem the criticism by offering a justification for
Cummings's actions. This took place on the bank holiday Monday, 25 May.

As noted in Section 1, the Cummings's press conference does not fit directly
within a pre-existing genre of communicative act, particularly in terms of the
combination of participant and setting. There was media comment around the

choice of the Downing Street garden for the event, as this location is usually reserved for hosting visitors of note (Helm and McKie, 2020) rather than for personal statements by advisors. Furthermore, as the co-leader of the Green Party, Jonathan Bartley (2020), complained in a letter to the Cabinet Secretary, it is general convention that 'Special advisers must not take public part in political controversy, through any form of statement whether in speeches or letters to the press, or in books, social media, articles or leaflets'. As with the argument over Trump's use of the White House for his RNC acceptance speech, the allegations here were that the government was using official symbols for partisan political reasons and thus violating established chronotopic precedents.

There were also number of other notable points relating to setting which differ from conventional presentation, and which accrue meaning from the distinct persona that has been constructed in the media for Dominic Cummings (see Figure 3). For instance, unlike all the men presenting at the daily Covid briefings, Cummings was not wearing a suit and tie, he sat at a small table rather than standing, and thus projected a far more informal image that one might typically expect for an official statement. He also arrived very late, which was additionally seen as a sign of a dismissive attitude to traditional decorum. But whereas a formality of dress and stance may be an index of seriousness and add to the sense of authority of the speaker under normal circumstances, the image of Cummings built by the media was of a maverick (e.g., Jones, 2020)

Figure 3 Dominic Cummings's statement to the press

who is frequently dismissive of convention, both in his dress sense and in his approach to the work of government, and these indexical details thus maintained this identity.

Other than these points, however, the general format was that of a standard press conference, with the chief actor giving a prepared statement, and then fielding questions from the news media, all of which was broadcast live via television and the internet. (It drew a very substantial audience of 3.7 million in fact [McGonagle, 2020].) Outside of the setting provided for the event, and these small points of presentation, the indexicals of authority and trust were mostly conveyed via the text of the speech itself, and particularly the way in which Cummings framed his account as a narrative, and in doing so, attempted to counter the critical interpretation that had been building in the press about his actions. This is looked at in further detail below.

Narrating a Story

There are two specific issues in terms of the narrative framing of the explanation which were used to index truthfulness and trustworthiness, but which in fact had the effect of achieving quite the opposite. These relate to character motivation and causality between events (Seargeant, 2020). At the heart of any dramatic narrative is some form of emotional motivation which acts as the driver for human behaviour (Westen, 2007). The government's response to the initial press reports was to justify Cummings's actions by foregrounding one emotional rationale over another. He may have stretched the rules ever so slightly by travelling to his parents' farm 264 miles away, they acknowledged, but he did so in order to ensure the safety of his infant son, thus satisfying a higher moral code.

This narrative used by government ministers and spokespeople was expressed in such a way that it was suggested Cummings should, in fact, be deserving of respect given his motivations, whereas those criticising him should be berated for failing to show the same devotion to their own families. For instance, Boris Johnson, at the press briefing of 24 May, stated that he thought Cummings 'followed the instincts of every father and every parent and I don't mark him down for that' (Tolhurst and Johnston, 2020).

Cummings's own statement on 25 May repeats this theme. It is not merely a report on his actions, but an explanation of the motivations for these, with a stress on his state of mind and thought processes at the time. Actions are thus framed in terms of their emotional motivation and causal significance, with the frequent appending of phrases such as 'I was worried ... '; 'My tentative conclusion ... ' which provide justification for his decision-making processes.

He regularly refers explicitly to his responsibilities as a father and husband and legitimises his actions through rationalisations based on these underlying responsibilities: 'there was nobody in London that we could reasonably ask to look after our child'; 'I was worried about the possibility of leaving my wife and child at home all day and off into the night'. This is supplemented with similarly ethical justification stemming from his sense of duty as a key member of the government support staff: 'I believe that in all circumstances I behaved reasonably and legally, balancing the safety of my family and the extreme situation in No.10 and the public interest in effective government to which I could contribute' (Cummings, 2020). Unlike Boris Johnson's performance in the first Covid press briefing, therefore, where the Prime Minister positioned himself as representative of the office rather than as an individual, Cummings is positioning himself as an individual citizen acting upon duties from within his personal life as well as his role as servant of the government.

The problem for both Cummings and the government, however, was that the specifics of this narrative sat within a larger narrative which had been a fundamental part of the political mainstream in the UK over the past several years, and which both Boris Johnson and Dominic Cummings had made central to their own political careers. This is the populist narrative that argues that a corrupt and self-serving elite is threatening the wellbeing of the ordinary people, and that the populist leader has emerged to right this wrong. The political personas of both Johnson and Cummings, indexed in details such as their everyday dress sense (and, in Boris Johnson's case, his wayward hair), their attitudes towards formal convention and their disregard for advice such as that on shaking hands, embody this narrative, casting the two men as outsiders or mavericks who, in siding with the general populace, feel it their duty to confront the corruption and ineffectiveness of the institutional elite.

Within this context, however, the trip to Durham immediately became a symbol of hypocrisy (Butler, 2020), undermining the 'Stay Home, Protect the NHS, Save Lives' story and its underpinning adage that the citizens of the nation were 'all in this together'. Instead, it suggested that those at the heart of government felt themselves to be above the law, and able to act in the way all self-serving politicians are likely to act. Cummings did attempt to acknowledge the conflict between this underlying narrative (and the values it embodied) and the perception that had built up of his actions, stating that the purpose of the press conference was because 'I wanted to explain what I thought, what I did and why, over this period, because I think that people like me who helped to make the rules should be accountable for their actions'. But as media and public reaction was to show, the performance in the press conference, especially in terms of the way he attempted to explain away rather than admit to and apologise for his actions, did little to placate the criticism of him (Horton, 2020).

The second way in which the narrative framing proved to be problematic rather than advantageous was in the way it committed Cummings to a coherent set of causally related decisions which structured his actions. One of the fundamental elements of the classic conception of narrative is that it relies on a clear pattern of causality, and expectations of this are what creates a convincing, and legally plausible (Green, 2020), story. In his statement, therefore, Cummings took care to justify each and every one of his decisions, relating them back to the motivations of family responsibility and civic duty. The result was an attempt to retrospectively construct a plausible story from a collection of disparate facts, particularly those which had already been revealed by the newspapers, along with the various sightings that members of the public had had of him. All the recorded sightings are listed in the explanation he gave at the press conference and are woven into a detailed timeline of events which, once again, are linked to particular motivations for the actions.

In attempting to account for all the facts within a causally coherent narrative in which actions are related to the specified motivations, the narration creates some very awkward scenarios. The most notable example of this was when he explained that, due to the fact his 'wife was very worried, particularly given my eyesight seemed to have been affected by the disease', they decided 'that we should go for a short drive to see if I could drive safely. We drove for roughly half an hour and ended up on the outskirts of Barnard Castle town'. While this account managed to provide an explanation for why he had been spotted at this location on this particular date, and thus give a *logical* motivation for his actions, it did not provide a *plausible* motivation for them as far as his critics were concerned (Parveen, 2020). In the end, the complexities of this counter-narrative had the result of simply highlighting the straight-forward emotional power of the original story put forward by the news media, namely that Cummings had broken the rules that the rest of the country were valiantly trying to stick with.

Despite the overwhelmingly negative reaction to Dominic Cummings's statement – the detail about his driving to Barnard Castle to ensure that his eyesight was not adversely affected by his illness became a long-running satirical meme (Horton, 2020) – the Prime Minster did not fire him, and he remained a prominent member of the government team for several months (he finally left the job in November 2020). Prior to the lockdown, his status as an unelected, but extremely influential, voice at the heart of power had already been attracting criticism (Morris, 2020), and this was merely intensified by the symbolism of this incident and his subsequent political survival. This, in turn, undermined trust in Boris Johnson's judgement, and thus in his authority. It also appeared to have a direct, adverse effect on the success of their persuasion strategies. There was research in the immediate aftermath of the Cummings's press conference which suggested the saga had undermined the government's message, and during the three weeks following the revelations about the Cummings trip, people in England were less likely to adhere to lockdown regulations than people in Scotland and Wales were (Fancourt et al., 2020). As with the government's Covid briefings, the meaning, as interpreted by the media/public, was a result not simply of the verbal discourse delivered by Cummings during his press conference, but of the time- and place-specific context in which this was delivered. And it was the conflict between text and context which failed to index trustworthiness, and instead indexed its exact opposite.

5 The Select Committee

One Year On

Almost a year after his Downing Street press conference, another public explanation of the events around Dominic Cummings's trip to Durham emerged, this time in the context of the joint enquiry by the Health and Social Care Committee and Science and Technology Committee into lessons to be learned from the response to the pandemic UK Parliament (2020). This was, once again, a communication event with specific genre conventions and expectations, which was part parliamentary business, part public performance. There was a marked difference of purpose for this event compared to the other two however. It was not part of the government's communication strategy around Covid and was not designed to persuade the population over the official approach to the pandemic. Yet it provided details from one of the main actors of how the previous year's statement had been planned, the intentions behind the form it took and, importantly, an evaluative critique of how it worked as a piece of persuasion.

Of course, the evidence given to the select committee was also a public political performance and, as such, a form of persuasive discourse in its own right, albeit with its own distinct purpose. Of importance in this respect is that, by the time of the enquiry, Cummings had left his job with the government, and there was a certain animosity between him and the Prime Minister and other members of the Cabinet. Cummings had become an outspoken critic of Boris Johnson, often opining that his character was not suited to the job – the quote in Section 1 ('He lies – so blatantly, so naturally, so regularly') being a convincing example of this.

The persuasive purpose behind his evidence to the select committee thus had two main strands to it: justifying his own actions of the year before, along with the way he had explained them at the impromptu press conference; and arguing for the validity of his criticisms against former colleagues.

This latter point is again a significant difference from the other two events we have looked at. In the first two events we have a mostly united front. The politicians, medical and scientific experts at the Covid briefings were all speaking from predominantly the same script and delivering a coordinated message delivered with the paraphernalia of institutional authority making use of the media as mouthpiece. The occasions on which this was not the case, when medical professionals and politicians appeared to take divergent positions, were quickly highlighted in press coverage. Compliance from the public was sought through the introduction of coercive measures, but these were sold to the population via persuasive strategies evoking shared values.

The second event was also very much a coordinated affair. Although Cummings was the only actor in the performance, consent to use the Downing Street garden as the location indicated the support of the Prime Minister, and behind-the-scenes discussions had clearly shaped the form that the event took. One year on, however, and this attempt at a united front had been abandoned. Dominic Cummings gave a further account of his actions the previous spring which dramatically changed the narrative and shed light on how the press conference had been devised as an act of persuasion and why, in his opinion, it had failed in its aims.

Lessons Learnt

The enquiry was set up in order to reflect upon the government's response to the pandemic and to fill the gap before a Public Inquiry, which had been promised by the Prime Minister for some unspecified future date, would take place. The stated aim of the enquiry was to

> use the independence of our cross-party committees and weekly detailed questioning of witnesses to consider the decisions taken and the evidence they were based on and assess their effectiveness. We will develop clear recommendations so that the UK can benefit from the lessons learned for future stages of this pandemic and for future crises. (UK Parliament, 2020)

In other words, it was intended to evaluate the effectiveness of the government's response to the pandemic by reflecting on the *process* of leadership within the context of the results achieved by that leadership. Embracing this stated aim of the committee, Cummings was to say during his evidence that 'this is a case study of how not to handle something like this' and conclude that

'The whole thing was a complete disaster. It undermined public confidence in the whole thing'. His testimony became, in effect, a form of self-critique reviewing the decisions and dynamics that resulted in his press conference in the Downing Street garden. But he also used this mea culpa as a vehicle for attacking the government's communication strategy: as he put it in his summative statement, 'We [he and the Prime Minister] both made a right Horlicks' of it all ('Horlicks' here being a slang term for making a complete mess of something).

In looking at his evidence to the joint committee we can thus approach it with two distinct questions in mind: What does his account say of how the previous account was designed as a piece of persuasion? And how is this account structured as a piece of persuasion in its own right?

The Art of Saying Sorry

The theme of Cummings's evidence was that he was here to justify his actions by providing a revised narrative of the relevant events: 'I think I should probably explain some things about this that were not put into the public domain at the time' (House of Commons, 2021a, 2021b). And that while mistakes had been made, those mistakes were to do with strategy rather than lapses in ethical behaviour. In terms of overall style, his tone was unreservedly apologetic throughout, emphatic-ally asserting, for example, that, 'I made a terrible, terrible, terrible mistake, which I am extremely sorry about', and 'I can only apologise for the whole debacle'. Yet in each case, the subject of these apologies was the unsuccessful communications strategy rather than the breaking lockdown of regulations. He was sorry for the way things had turned out rather than for the trip to Durham itself, and for the adverse implications he felt it had had on the government's ability to persuade the populace rather than for any perceived ethical violation on his part. When prompted by one of the MPs on the panel to consider an apology for the actions themselves rather than the way they had been spun ('I think the nation just wanted to hear one three-word statement from you: "I am sorry"') Cummings evaded the point by insisting that his behaviour at the time had been 'reasonable'. This particular word was regularly repeated throughout his testimony ('I think that my behaviour in leaving London at the time was perfectly reasonable, and other people … agreed with me that it was reasonable for me to move my family'), offering an explanation based on what he was putting forward as expected norms of behaviour for someone in his circum-stances. For the Conservative MP Dean Russell, however, the public at that time was not concerned with what might be reasonable or not. Public perception was shaped by an emotional response to the effects of the pandemic, by the 'real, sheer emotion of the country at the time' which led to '1,000 emails in my constituency mailbox from people who were really angry about this'.

Russell also introduced the concept of responsibility, and distinguished between three types: Cummings's personal responsibility, the media's role and 'Government's responsibility for looking after the people who are being representative and making these tough decisions in a world emergency'. He also highlighted the importance of notions of trust – trust both in the messaging and in those communicating the message. Here again, the substance of Cummings's replies was on the persuasive responsibilities of the government and how they had been founding wanting. A number of the questions to Cummings were, in fact, framed in such a way to explicitly highlight the suggestions that the incident from the year before had had a negative effect on the government's communication strategy. Luke Evans, the Conservative MP for Bosworth in Leicestershire, for example, spoke of 'a certain infamous trip [to Barnard Castle] and that had huge influence on how people perceived the lockdown', to which Cummings replied that the 'whole episode was definitely a major disaster for the Government and for the covid policy' in that it undermined trust in, and thus the authority of those fronting the communications strategy.

As in the previous year's account, Cummings made much of the timeline in which events occurred, and how each decision was contingent on a previous incident. The information about the motivation behind his movements which had not previously been in the public domain related to security threats that had forced his family the previous year to move out of their house for a number of weeks, he said. Various threats to his family then occurred in February 2020 – that is, before the start of lockdown – and then again in March just as lockdown was coming into force. This was the background context for moving his family to Durham, he explained, and was also the reason why the police had spoken to him while he was staying up there. His explanation then was that the narrative as he had related it in 2020 was based on facts, but that consequential details had been omitted, thus creating an ultimately false impression of what actually happened: 'what I said was true, but we left out a crucial part of it all.' The main thrust of his testimony was not about whether the government communications had been truthful or not, but rather whether they had been effective.

6 Conclusion: Embodied Indexical Communication in Leadership Contexts

'Herd' Mentality

Boris Johnson's spell as Prime Minister eventually came to an untimely end due to a loss of confidence by – or a rebellion from – MPs in his own party, following what was seen as the mishandling of the situation over sexual harassment allegations about the Deputy Chief Whip Christopher Pincher. This controversy came close on the heels of the various 'partygate' scandals and shared many of the same elements, particularly accusations that the Prime Minister had not been wholly truthful in disclosing what he knew and when he knew it.

In his resignation speech, and a month later in his farewell speech outside Downing Street, Johnson made pointed comments about the way power was managed when it comes to choosing and supporting a leader in politics. In the first of these two speeches he referred to the process as Darwinian ('our brilliant and Darwinian system' [Gov.uk, 2022b]), presumably a metaphor, in this instance, for the ruthlessness of self-interest needed to survive in the political gene pool. He also talked of the 'herd' mentality which constitutes the support that any leader needs to command in order to keep hold of the reins of power ('as we've seen at Westminster, the herd is powerful and when the herd moves, it moves' [Gov.uk, 2022b]). The 'herd' metaphor implies an absence of rationality when it comes to decision making and was certainly interpreted by some commentators in the media as an expression of rebuke to his parliamentary colleagues (Ferguson, 2022).

By the time of his farewell speech, some weeks later, he had adjusted his rhetoric slightly, and now referred to the role of leader of the party as part of a relay race – although, still very pointedly, he complained that the rules of this race had been changed halfway through its running ('they changed the rules half-way through but never mind that now' [Gov.uk, 2022a]).

Each of these metaphors frames the leader's status as something which is dependent on the whims of others, and which is difficult, if not impossible, to successfully manage if the political winds are against you. Of the three, 'herd' is perhaps the most revealing. To describe the fortunes of the leader as being dependent on the 'Darwinian' nature of the political environment is simply to acknowledge that intrigue and ego are among the central elements of that environment. To complain that the rules have been changed mid-game is to have a seemingly naïve idea about how rules operate in an environment that's run on intrigue and ego. The metaphor of the 'herd', however, suggests that the management of public opinion is absolutely central to surviving in politics, and that this opinion can appear capricious and thus needs careful and continuous handling.

Embodied Indexical Communication

By the spring of 2022, a few months before Johnson's resignation, when there were local elections for councils across the UK, 'partygate' was mostly being framed as a general instance of political hypocrisy rather than as something which damaged the authority of the communications strategy on Covid. The media discourse was focused on 'cunning leadership', the idea that the aim of those in power is to retain that power (James, 2015a, 2015b), and a constant theme in the press was whether Boris Johnson would survive as Prime Minister.

A number of things are noticeable about the type of political communication we have looked at in this book. The first is the fact that it can seemingly be derailed by perceived mistakes much more swiftly than the sense of trust upon which it relies can be built up. In the case of the events discussed in the book, the revelations about Cummings's trip to Durham as they were reported and explained over the weekend of the 22 and 23 May 2020 quickly came to dominate discussion of the government's handling of the pandemic at the time, and particularly raised questions about the Prime Minister's decision-making in relation to his unqualified support for his special advisor. This, arguably, undermined the message that had been being nurtured since the first Covid briefing on 16 March. The way this played out was partly the result of the mediated nature of modern leadership. The media tends not merely to report the actions of the leader, but to provide analysis and commentary on them, which has the effect of constructing a narrative around any and all perceived deficiencies. This narrative need not be a negative one, of course, and its complexion will be dependent on the ideological stance of the news organisation. But leadership is very much framed as embodied in the person of the leader – in their utterances, their actions and their character – and is thus reliant on a form of embodied indexical communication.

Figure 4 outlines the five stages of how embodied indexical communication applies to perceptions of leadership in politics and how it operates as a contributing factor to voice and to the factors which confer upon an utterance a level of pragmatic force. Stage 1 comprises the traits, behaviour or action which conveys indexical meaning. For instance, Boris Johnson's dishevelled appearance and unkempt hair, his rhetorical idiosyncrasies and proneness to what the press tend to refer to as 'gaffes' flout the normal decorum and conventions of political conduct (Stage 2). In Johnson's case, however, flouting conventions plays to the narrative of a maverick character who is unafraid of taking an antagonistic stance towards established norms – despite, of course, being an almost archetypal product of establishment institutions himself (Stage 3). In the past, the media has written flatteringly about this persona and devoted plenty of coverage to Johnson's various antics (Stage 4) which has contributed to his generally high profile and, for a long while prior to his actually becoming leader, led to speculation about his one day becoming Prime Minister. When the opportunity arose with the resignation of Theresa May in 2019, he was thus well positioned to win the leadership election (Stage 5).

Embodied indexical communication in political leadership

Embodied traits which act as indexicals	Relationship to normative values	Significance of this relationship for leadership narrative	Media commentary on the significance of and stylistic choices used to communicate this	Effects of this media commentary within the workings of the political system
Including : · appearance and bearing · behaviour · speech · actions	cultural expectations of appropriate deportment, as determined by the genre of the event, based on convention or tradition	to what extent conformity to or neglect of these accords with the narrative which underpins the persona of the politician	how instances of the display of these traits are highlighted by the press, and the interpretation given to them	how this media narrative impacts on the leader's status as this is determined by the evaluative mechanisms offered by the political system

Figure 4 Embodied indexical communication in political leadership

All of this then provided background context for the government's approach to communication during the Covid crisis that has been discussed in the sections above.

Authority and Leadership

We started with the contention that power can be defined as the ability to get people to do things they do not necessarily wish to do; that compliance through persuasion is often preferable to the use of coercion, especially in societies which subscribe to liberal democratic ideals; and that persuasion is a particular type of communication which involves communicating a convincing message. The 'convincing' element of this formula can be created in various ways, amongst which are drawing on a sense of authority and developing trust. Definitions of leadership are broader than it simply being the ability or oppor-tunity to exercise power as conceptualised above, of course. But in situations such as a pandemic, where the need arises to curtail people's rights as part of the strategy for coping with the spread of the disease, this definition provides a good starting point for analysing leadership approaches.

The aim of the book has then been to give an account of the way that an important aspect of political leadership is founded on the communication of certain key values which provide the grounds for messaging which aims to influence the behaviour of the public. In a context such as the response to a pandemic, authority over both information (the integrity of available scientific knowledge) and action (clear and coherent guidelines of behaviour), which itself is dependent on trust (a belief in the sincerity and integrity of those conveying the information and advice), are key values which give weight to the government's voice, and help translate intent into action. This context is constructed by various semiotic means, which are communicated at a particular time and place and draw on traditions and values in society ranging from the immediate and local to the enduring and national. Moreover, the specific context always exists within wider, dynamic contexts (also situated within time and place), and public interpretation of the messaging will respond to this holistic context, particularly as it is filtered and repeated by the media. To gauge how this works it is necessary to look beyond simply the rhetoric used by leaders when communicating, and to consider the act of communication from a holistic perspective.

In the case of Boris Johnson government's handling of the Covid crisis during the spring of 2020, a noticeable amount of the criticism which led to a loss of public trust and thus to a diminishing sense of authority can be seen to arise from violations of expectations which the government itself had set up in presenting an image of authoritative and trustworthy leadership: foregrounding the import-ance of following expert scientific opinion and then removing experts from the briefing format; preaching a communal response predicated on national sacri-fices then having it revealed that a key government official had taken a seemingly individualistic response which defied the values that underpinned the national response and then followed this up with plausibly dubious explan-ations to justify his actions.

It was reversals such as these which ruptured the very context that had been created to give significance to the messaging, and which then caused an undermining of the messaging. And it was in this sense that control of the crisis appeared to descend into a state of chaos, as clear and coherent lines of communication were disrupted by a failure to navigate the dynamic nature of the political and cultural environment. As has been argued throughout, messa-ging is always reliant on how, when and where it is communicated, all of which contributes to a sense of voice and the government's rhetoric being perceived as meaningful and persuasive. It is notable that despite the mantra of being 'led by the science', the Johnson premiership was judged ultimately not on the rational arguments it made in enacting and justifying a quarantine policy (once the initial complacency of the response had been overcome), but instead via an emotional reaction on the part of the media and public to the Prime Minister's behaviour and the 'message' that this sent about his altitude to the responsibilities of the office.

In retrospect, a case study centred around Boris Johnson's premiership provides examples of various factors which contribute to modern ideas of political leadership. His leadership role was removed from him when he lost the support of his parliamentary colleagues. Whatever the actual motivations for this withdrawal of support, the result was facilitated by the specifics of the UK parliamentary system and, just as his election as leader had not involved a vote by the public at large, neither did his forced resignation. Stated motivations for this withdrawal of support were that he had lied about his actions and was thus not morally deserving of support, and that he was now no longer an asset but a liability to the fortunes of the Conservative Party (Mason and Dugan, 2022). The latter of these relates to ideas of cunning leadership, the former to inspirational leadership. But both reflect a belief that his ability to persuade the electorate was no longer sufficient for the challenges the party faced in leading the country through a period of crisis.

References

Agha, A. (2007) *Language and Social Relations*, Cambridge: Cambridge University Press.

Alon, I., Farrell, M. and Li, S. (2020) Regime type and COVID-19 response, *FIIB Business Review*, 9: 3, pp. 152–60.

Amsler, M. and Shore, C. (2017) Responsibilisation and leadership in the neoliberal university: A New Zealand perspective, *Discourse: Studies in the Cultural Politics of Education*, 38: 1, pp. 123–37.

Aspinall, E. (2022) COVID-19 timeline, *British Foreign Policy Group*, 8 April, https://bfpg.co.uk/2020/04/covid-19-timeline/ (accessed 5 November 2022).

Avolio, B. J. (2004) *Leadership Development in Balance: MADE/Born*, New York: Psychology Press.

Bakhtin, M. M. (1981) Forms of time and of the chronotope in the novel, in Holquist, M. (ed.) *The Dialogic Imagination: Four Essays*, Austin: University of Texas Press, pp. 84–258.

Baldwin, P. (2021) *Fighting the First Wave: Why the Coronavirus was Tackled so Differently Across the Globe*, Cambridge: Cambridge University Press.

Ball, J. (2017) *Post-truth: How Bullshit Conquered the World*, London: Biteback.

Ball, S. (1988) *Baldwin and the Conservative Party: The Crisis of 1929–1931*, Connecticut, NH: Yale University Press.

Bartley, J. (2020) Letter to Sir Mark Philip Sedwill, Cabinet Secretary, *Green Party*, 26 May, www.greenparty.org.uk/assets/files/letters/Letter-to-Mark-Sedwill-260520-Jonathan-Bartley.pdf (accessed 14 August 2020).

Batchelor, T. (2021) Eleven arrested as protesters clash with police outside parliament on 'Freedom Day', *The Independent*, 19 July, www.independent.co.uk/news/uk/home-news/covid-freedom-day-protest-westminster-b1886671.html (accessed 14 August 2021).

BBC News (2020) Coronavirus: Daily Downing Street press conference scrapped, 23 June, www.bbc.co.uk/news/uk-politics-53155905 (accessed 14 August 2020).

Bermingham, R. (2020) Media, communications and COVID-19: What are experts concerned about? *UK Parliament*, 21 May, https://post.parliament.uk/media-communications-and-covid-19-what-are-experts-concerned-about/ (accessed 5 November 2022).

Block, E. and Negrine, R. (2017) The populist communication style: Toward a critical framework, *International Journal of Communication Systems*, 11, pp. 178–97.

Blommaert, J. (2005) *Discourse: A Critical Introduction*, Cambridge: Cambridge University Press.

Blommaert, J. and De Fina, A. (2017) Chronotopic identities: On the timespace organization of who we are, in De Fina, A., Ikizoglu, D. and Wegner, J. (eds.) *Diversity and Super-Diversity: Sociocultural Linguistic Perspectives*, Washington, DC: Georgetown University Press, pp. 1–15.

Bowcott, O., Quinn, B. and Carrell, S. (2019) Johnson's suspension of parliament unlawful, supreme court rules, *The Guardian*, 24 September, www .theguardian.com/law/2019/sep/24/boris-johnsons-suspension-of-parliament-unlawful-supreme-court-rules-prorogue (accessed 14 August 2021).

Brettschneider, C. (2010) When the state speaks, what should it say? The dilemmas of freedom of expression and democratic persuasion, *Perspectives on Politics*, 8: 4, pp. 1005–19.

Butler, J. (2020) Cummings is the symbol of a political class that knows consequences are for little people, *The Guardian*, 28 May, www.theguardian .com/commentisfree/2020/may/28/dominic-cummings-democracy-laws-truth-consequences (accessed 14 August 2021).

Cabinet Office (2011) The Cabinet Manual: A guide to laws, conventions and rules on the operation of government, https://assets.publishing.service.gov .uk/government/uploads/system/uploads/attachment_data/file/60641/cabinet-manual.pdf (accessed 14 August 2021).

Calvert, J., Arbuthnott, G. and Leake, J. (2020) Coronavirus: 38 days when Britain sleepwalked into disaster, *The Times*, 19 April, www.thetimes.co.uk/ article/coronavirus-38-days-when-britain-sleepwalked-into-disaster-hq3b9tlgh (accessed 14 August 2020).

Channel 4 (2020) 'Stop non-essential contact with others': UK government virus update, *YouTube*, 16 March, www.youtube.com/watch?v=QTZwbEoDC1c (accessed 14 August 2020).

Charteris-Black, J. (2019) *Metaphors of Brexit: No Cherries on the Cake?* London: Palgrave Macmillan.

Clifton, J., Schnurr, S. and Van De Mieroop, D. (2019) *The Language of Leadership Narratives: A Social Practice Perspective*, Abingdon: Routledge.

Collins, P. (2021) Boris Johnson is a liar and a chancer, but popular. Why? *New Statesman*, 21 July, www.newstatesman.com/politics/2021/07/boris-johnson-liar-and-chancer-popular-why (accessed 14 July 2021).

Constant, B. (2003 [1815]) *Principles of Politics Applicable to All Governments*, trans. N. Capaldi, Carmel, IN: Liberty Fund.

Crossley, S. (2007) A chronotopic approach to genre analysis: An exploratory study, *English for Specific Purposes*, 26: 1, pp. 4–24.

Cummings, D. (2020) Full transcript of Boris Johnson aide's statement from Downing Street, *The Independent*, 25 May, www.independent.co.uk/news/uk/politics/dominic-cummings-statement-speech-transcript-durham-full-text-read-lockdown-a9531856.html (accessed 14 August 2020).

Cummings, D. (2021) Substack, 5 July, https://dominiccummings.substack.com (accessed 14 July 2021).

Dahl, R. A. (1957) The concept of power, *Behavioural Science*, 2: 3, pp. 201–15.

Daily Mail U.K. (@DailyMailUK) (2022) Wednesday's @DailyMailUK #MailFrontPages, *Twitter*, 12 April, https://twitter.com/DailyMailUK/status/1513994827595235328.

De Fina, A. (2019) Insights and challenges of chronotopic analysis for sociolinguistics, in Kroon, S. and Swanenberg, J. (eds.) *Chronotopic Identity Work: Sociolinguistic Analyses of Cultural and Linguistic Phenomena in Time and Space*, Bristol: Multilingual Matters, pp. 193–203.

Devlin, K. (2020) 'It was essential: No 10 breaks silence to defend Dominic Cummings' 250-mile trip during lockdown, *The Independent*, 23 May, www.independent.co.uk/news/uk/politics/dominic-cummings-coronavirus-lockdown-trip-no-10-latest-a9529461.html (accessed 14 August 2020).

Eglene, O., Dawes, S. S. and Schneider, C. A. (2007) Authority and leadership patterns in public sector knowledge networks, *The American Review of Public Administration*, 37: 1, pp.91–113.

Ellul, J. (1973) *Propaganda: The Formation of Men's Attitudes*, New York: Random House.

Esser, F. and Strömbäck, J. (eds.) (2014) *Mediatization of Politics: Understanding the Transformation of Western Democracies*, London: Palgrave Macmillan.

Etzioni, A. (1964) *Modern Organizations*, London: Prentice Hall.

Fancourt, D., Steptoe, A. and Wright, L. (2020) The Cummings effect: Politics, trust, and behaviours during the COVID-19 pandemic, *The Lancet*, 396: 10249, pp. 464–5.

Ferguson, E. (2022) Boris Johnson announcement: Live updates as PM resigns and blames MPs for 'herd' mentality in bullish speech, *i News*, 7 July, https://inews.co.uk/news/politics/boris-johnson-announcement-live-updates-prime-minister-resigns-downing-street-statement-1728927 (accessed 5 November 2022).

Fetzer, A. and Bull, P. (2012) Doing leadership in political speech: Semantic processes and pragmatic inferences, *Discourse & Society*, 23, pp. 127–44.

Finnis, A. (2020) Coronavirus latest: Government delay in imposing lockdown blamed for steep rise in Covid-19 cases, *i Paper*, 24 May, https://inews.co.uk/news/coronavirus-latest-government-delay-imposing-lockdown-430742 (accessed 14 August 2020).

Fitzgerald, M. (2021) Boris Johnson and his government are attacking press freedom: We must not let them win, *Open Democracy*, 2 February, www.opendemocracy.net/en/boris-johnson-and-his-government-are-attacking-press-freedom-we-must-not-let-them-win/ (accessed 5 November 2022).

Freedland, J. (2020) PM finally defers to experts as he deflects tricky Covid questions, *The Guardian*, 16 March, www.theguardian.com/politics/2020/mar/16/johnson-finally-defers-to-experts-as-he-deflects-tricky-covid-questions (accessed 5 November 2022).

Goffman, E. (1990 [1959]) *The Presentation of Self in Everyday Life*, London: Penguin.

Gov.uk (2020a) Coronavirus (COVID-19), www.gov.uk/coronavirus (accessed 14 August 2020).

Gov.uk (2020b) Prime Minister's statement on coronavirus (COVID-19), 16 March, www.gov.uk/government/speeches/pm-statement-on-corona virus-16-march-2020 (accessed 14 August 2020).

Gov.uk (2022a) Boris Johnson's final speech as Prime Minister, 6 September, www.gov.uk/government/speeches/boris-johnsons-final-speech-as-prime-minister-6-september-2022 (accessed 5 November 2022).

Gov.uk (2022b) Prime Minister Boris Johnson's statement in Downing Street, 7 July, www.gov.uk/government/speeches/prime-minister-boris-johnsons-statement-in-downing-street-7-july-2022 (accessed 5 November 2022).

Green, D. A. (2020) Dominic Cummings's statement: A guided tour, *Financial Times*, 27 May, www.ft.com/video/e82b5a00-3ad5-4d2c-9703-ff14942aa5b1 (accessed 14 August 2020).

Grint, K. (2005) *Leadership: Limits and Possibilities*, Basingstoke: Palgrave Macmillan.

Gupta, S. (2022) *Political Catchphrases and Contemporary History*, Oxford: Oxford University Press.

Hackman, M. Z. and Johnson, C. E. (2013) *Leadership: A Communication Perspective*, Long Grove, IL: Waveland Press.

Hamrick, E. S. (2020) Re: Hatch Act advisory on convention acceptance speech at the White House, *U.S. Office of Special Counsel*, 12 August, https://republicans-oversight.house.gov/wp-content/uploads/2020/08/AO-re-Convention-speech-at-WH.pdf (accessed 14 August 2020).

Hassan, A. and Ahmed, F. (2011) Authentic leadership, trust and work engagement, *International Journal of Human and Social Sciences*, 6: 3, pp. 164–70.

Helm, T. and McKie, R. (2020) From rose garden to ridicule: How a week of disaster for Tories and Dominic Cummings unfolded, *The Observer*, 30 May, www.theguardian.com/politics/2020/may/30/from-rose-garden-to-ridicule-how-a-week-of-disaster-for-tories-and-dominic-cummings-unfolded (accessed 14 August 2020).

Hennessy, P. (1998) *The Prime Minister: The Office and its Holders since 1945*, London: Allen Lane.

Hickman, A. (2020) PR pros lambast new government 'Stay alert' slogan as 'unclear' and 'unhelpful', *PR Weekly*, 12 May, www.prweek.com/article/1682781/pr-pros-lambast-new-government-stay-alert-slogan-unclear-unhelpful (accessed 14 August 2020).

Hope, C. and Dixon, H. (2020) The story behind 'Stay Home, Protect the NHS, Save Lives': The slogan that was too successful, *The Daily Telegraph*, 1 May, www.telegraph.co.uk/politics/2020/05/01/story-behind-stay-home-protect-nhs-save-lives/ (accessed 14 August 2020).

Hopkin, J. (2020) Brexit thinking poisoned the government's response to COVID-19, *LSE Blog*, 9 June, https://blogs.lse.ac.uk/brexit/2020/06/09/brexit-thinking-poisoned-the-governments-response-to-covid-19/ (accessed 14 August 2020).

Horti, S. (2020) The dangerous arrogance of the government's slow coronavirus response, *New Statesman*, 21 April, www.newstatesman.com/2020/04/dangerous-arrogance-governments-slow-coronavirus-response (accessed 14 August 2020).

Horton, H. (2020) Should have gone to Barnard Castle: Social media users mock Cummings trip to beauty spot, *The Telegraph*, 26 May, www.telegraph.co.uk/news/2020/05/26/should-have-gone-barnard-castle-social-media-users-mock-cummings/ (accessed 14 August 2020).

House of Commons (2021a) Oral evidence: Coronavirus: Lessons learnt, HC 95, *Health and Social Care Committee and Science and Technology Committee*, 26 May, https://committees.parliament.uk/oralevidence/2249/html/ (accessed 20 August 2021).

House of Commons (2021b) Wednesday 26 May video, *Science and Technology Committee and Health and Social Care Committee*, www.parliamentlive.tv/Event/Index/d919fbc9-72ca-42de-9b44-c0bf53a7360b/ (accessed 20 August 2021).

Hyland-Wood, B., Gardner, J., Leask, J. and Ecker, U. K. H. (2021) Toward effective government communication strategies in the era of COVID-19, *Humanities and Social Sciences Communications*, 8: 30, www.nature.com/articles/s41599-020-00701-w (accessed 5 November 2022).

Hymes, D. (1996) *Ethnography, Linguistics, Narrative Inequality: Towards and Understanding of Voice*, London: Taylor & Francis.

ITV (2020a) Coronavirus 'lockdown' leads Tuesday morning's papers as Britons prepare for 'life put on hold', 17 March, www.itv.com/news/2020-03-17/what-the-papers-say-march-17 (accessed 5 November 2022).

ITV (2020b) Dominic Cummings' Durham trip: Timeline of events as minister resigns over No 10 response, 26 May, www.itv.com/news/2020-05-26/dominic-cummings-durham-trip-timeline (accessed 14 August 2020).

ITV (2020c) Politicians from all sides wish Johnson well after PM admitted to hospital, 5 April, www.itv.com/news/2020-04-05/politicians-from-all-sides-wish-johnson-well-after-pm-admitted-to-hospital (accessed 14 August 2020).

James, T. (2015a) *British Conservative Leaders*, London: Biteback.

James, T. (2015b) *British Labour Leaders*, London: Biteback.

Johnston, J. (2020) *Media Relations: Issues & Strategies*, London: Routledge.

Jones, A. (2020) Dominic Cummings: The maverick outsider who has made a career out of sailing close to the wind, *The Daily Telegraph*, 24 May, www.telegraph.co.uk/politics/2020/05/24/dominic-cummings-maverick-outsider-has-made-career-sailing-close/ (accessed 14 August 2020).

Kellner, K. (2020) No. 10 is misreading the polls on lockdown, *Prospect*, 17 June, www.prospectmagazine.co.uk/politics/no-10-is-misreading-the-polls-on-lockdown-coronavirus-two-metre-rule-public-opinion.

Kettle, M. (2019) This is a Brexit election: But Boris Johnson will not get Brexit done, *The Guardian*, 12 December, www.theguardian.com/commentisfree/2019/dec/12/brexit-election-boris-johnson-tories (accessed 14 August 2020).

Krishna, R. (2020) Here is the transcript of what Boris Johnson said on This Morning about the new coronavirus, *Full Fact*, 10 March, https://fullfact.org/health/boris-johnson-coronavirus-this-morning/ (accessed 14 August 2020).

Kroon, S. and Swanenberg, J. (eds.) (2019) *Chronotopic Identity Work: Sociolinguistic Analyses of Cultural and Linguistic Phenomena in Time and Space*, Bristol: Multilingual Matters.

Landler, M. (2020) Taking a page from White House, Boris Johnson bets on live press briefings, *New York Times*, 26 October, www.nytimes.com/2020/10/26/world/europe/boris-johnson-allegra-stratton-live-media-briefings.html (accessed 14 August 2021).

Lasswell, H. D. (1928) The function of the propagandist, *International Journal of Ethics*, 38: 3, pp. 258–78.

Lawson, C. (2020) Did Trump officials commit violations of the Hatch Act during the RNC? An explainer, *The Dispatch*, 2 August, https://thedispatch.com/p/did-trump-officials-commit-violations (accessed 14 August 2020).

Luebke, S. M. (2021) Political authenticity: Conceptualization of a popular term, *The International Journal of Press/Politics*, 26: 3, pp. 635–53.

Mason, R. (2020) Boris Johnson boasted of shaking hands on day Sage warned not to, *The Guardian*, 5 May, www.theguardian.com/politics/2020/may/05/boris-johnson-boasted-of-shaking-hands-on-day-sage-warned-not-to (accessed 14 August 2020).

Mason, R. and Dugan, E. (2022) The Tory MPs who have quit Boris Johnson's government – listed, *The Guardian*, 6 July, www.theguardian.com/politics/2022/jul/06/the-tory-mps-who-have-quit-boris-johnsons-government-listed (accessed 5 November 2022).

Mautner, G. (2005) The entrepreneurial university: A discursive profile of a higher education buzzword, *Critical Discourse Studies*, 2: 2, pp. 95–120.

Mazza, E. (2020) 'Abomination': Critics rip Trump for 'Desecrating' White House with RNC speech, *Huffington Post*, 28 August, www.huffingtonpost.co.uk/entry/trump-white-house-desecration-2020-rnc_n_5f4868a9c5b64f17e13b1d3e (accessed 14 August 2020).

McGonagle, S. (2020) At a time when new drama or documentary is a rarity, the Dominic Cummings interview is welcome television viewing, *Irish News*, 30 May, www.irishnews.com/lifestyle/tvandradio/2020/05/30/news/at-a-time-when-new-drama-or-documentary-is-a-rarity-the-dominic-cummings-interview-is-welcome-television-viewing-1955208/ (accessed 14 August 2020).

McIntosh, S. (2022) I'm a celebrity: Matt Hancock told breaking Covid rules was 'slap in face', *BBC News*, 11 November, www.bbc.co.uk/news/entertainment-arts-63591640 (accessed 11 November 2022).

McMyler, B. (2011) *Testimony, Trust, and Authority*, Oxford: Oxford University Press.

McTague, T. (2021) Boris Johnson knows exactly what he's doing, *The Atlantic*, July/August, www.theatlantic.com/magazine/archive/2021/07/boris-johnson-minister-of-chaos/619010/ (accessed 14 July 2021).

Mills, T. (2016) *The BBC: Myth of a Public Service*, London: Verso.

The Mirror (@DailyMirror) (2022) Tomorrow's front page: Led by liars & lawbreakers, *Twitter*, 12 April, https://twitter.com/DailyMirror/status/1513993297106243592.

Morris, J. (2020) Dominic Cummings: The unelected official with enormous power in Downing Street, *Yahoo News*, 13 February, https://uk.news.yahoo.com/dominic-cummings-sajid-javid-resignation-152136002.html (accessed 14 August 2020).

Neustadt, R. E. (1991) *Presidential Power and the Modern Presidents: The Politics of Leadership from Roosevelt to Reagan*, New York: Free Press.

Osborne, P. (2021) *The Assault on Truth: Boris Johnson, Donald Trump and the Emergence of a New Moral Barbarism*, London: Simon and Schuster.

Oliver, C. (2020) Of Leviathan and lockdowns, *Politico*, 30 April, www.politico .eu/article/thomas-hobbesof-philosophy-coronavirus-leviathan-and-lock downs/ (accessed 14 July 2021).

Özdüzen, Ö., Ianosev, B. and Ozgul, B. A. (2021) Freedom or self-interest? Motivations, ideology and visual symbols uniting anti-lockdown protesters in the UK, *Political Studies Association*, 14 September, www.psa.ac.uk/psa/ news/freedom-or-self-interest-motivations-ideology-and-visual-symbols- uniting-anti-lockdown/ (accessed 5 November 2022).

Pagden, A. (2013) *The Enlightenment: And Why it Still Matters*, Oxford: Oxford University Press.

Partington, A. (2018) *The Language of Persuasion in Politics*, Abingdon: Routledge.

Parveen, N. (2020) The view from Barnard Castle: 'He's made a mockery of us', *The Guardian*, 28 May, www.theguardian.com/politics/2020/may/28/ view-from-barnard-castle-dominic-cummings-hes-made-a-mockery-of-us (accessed 5 November 2022).

Pennings, S. and Symons, X. (2021) Persuasion, not coercion or incentivisation, is the best means of promoting COVID-19 vaccination, *Journal of Medical Ethics*, 47, pp. 709–11.

Quinn, M. (2020) U.S. Office of Special Counsel says Trump can give convention speech at White House, *CBS News*, 13 August, www.cbsnews.com/news/ trump-nomination-acceptance-speech-republican-national-convention-white- house/ (accessed 14 August 2020).

Sanders, K. B. (2020) British government communication during the 2020 COVID-19 pandemic: Learning from high reliability organizations, *Church, Communication and Culture*, 5: 3, pp.356–77.

Schultz, J. (1998) *Reviving the Fourth Estate: Democracy, Accountability and the Media*, Cambridge: Cambridge University Press.

Seargeant, P. (2020) *The Art of Political Storytelling: Why Stories Win Votes in Post-truth Politics*, London: Bloomsbury.

Seargeant, P. (2022) Complementary concepts of disinformation: Conspiracy theories and 'fake news', in Demata, M., Zorzi, V. and Zottola, A. (eds.) *Conspiracy Theory Discourses*, Amsterdam: John Benjamins.

Seargeant, P. (2023) Opposition narratives to tax-cut advocacy, *Unchecked*.

Seldon, A., Thoms, I. and Meakin, J. (2021) *The Impossible Office? The History of the British Prime Minister*, Cambridge: Cambridge University Press.

Severgnini, C. (2020) Coronavirus: Primi due casi in Italia, *Corriere della sera*, 31 January, www.corriere.it/cronache/20_gennaio_30/coronavirus-italia- corona-9d6dc436-4343-11ea-bdc8-faf1f56f19b7.shtml (accessed 14 August 2021).

Shaub, W. (@waltshaub) (2020) This abomination may be ..., *Twitter*, 28 August, https://twitter.com/waltshaub/status/1299162605345550336?s=21.

Siltaoja, M. (2009) On the discursive construction of a socially responsible organization, *Scandinavian Journal of Management*, 25: 2, pp. 191–202.

Silverstein, M. (1976) Shifters, linguistic categories and cultural description, in Basso, K. H. and Selby, H. A. (eds.) *Meaning in Anthropology*, Albuquerque: University of New Mexico Press, pp. 11–55.

Silverstein, M. (2003) Indexical order and the dialectics of sociolinguistic life, *Language and Communication*, 23, pp. 193–229.

Spence, N. (2020) When Simon Binns, editor of LADbible, asked a question during the daily government Coronavirus briefing last weekend it sparked surprise, *PR Weekly*, 14 April, www.prweek.com/article/1680233/why-surprised-ladbible-daily-covid-19-press-briefings (accessed 14 August 2020).

Syal, R. (2020) Chief nurse was dropped from briefings after refusing to back Cummings, *The Guardian*, 20 July, www.theguardian.com/politics/2020/jul/20/englands-chief-nurse-dropped-from-covid-19-briefing-after-refusing-to-back-cummings-ruth-may (accessed 14 August 2021).

Tolhurst, A. and Johnston, J. (2020) Boris Johnson says Dominic Cummings 'acted legally, responsibly and with integrity' in lockdown row, *Politics Home*, 24 May, www.politicshome.com/news/article/boris-johnson-says-dominic-cummings-acted-legally-responsibly-and-with-integrity-in-lock down-row (accessed 14 August 2020).

Tominey, C. (2020) Dominic Cummings: The vote leave svengali who has made himself untouchable in Downing Street, *Daily Telegraph*, 23 May, www.telegraph.co.uk/politics/2020/05/23/dominic-cummings-vote-leave-svengali-has-made-untouchable-downing/ (accessed 26 October 2020).

Torrance, D. and Humes, W. (2015) The shifting discourses of educational leadership: International trends and Scotland's response, *Educational Management Administration and Leadership*, 43: 5, pp. 792–810.

UK Parliament (2020) Parliamentary committees join forces: Inquiry launched to scrutinise government response to the COVID-19 pandemic, https://committees.parliament.uk/committee/81/health-and-social-care-committee/news/119853/parliamentary-committees-join-forces-inquiry-launched-to-scrutinise-government-response-to-the-covid19-pandemic/ (accessed 20 August 2021).

Vos, T. P. and Thomas, R. J. (2018) The discursive construction of journalistic authority in a post-truth age, *Journalism Studies*, 19: 13, pp. 2001–10.

Walker, P. (2020) Boris Johnson missed five coronavirus Cobra meetings, Michael Gove says, *The Guardian*, 19 April, www.theguardian.com/world/

2020/apr/19/michael-gove-fails-to-deny-pm-missed-five-coronavirus-cobra-meetings (accessed 14 August 2020).

Warren, M. E. (2018) Trust and democracy, in Uslaner, E. M. (ed.) *The Oxford Handbook of Social and Political Trust*, Oxford: Oxford University Press, pp. 75–94.

Waterson, J., Proctor, K. and Robinson, G. (2020) Public to get question at daily UK coronavirus press conference, *The Guardian*, 27 April, www.theguardian.com/world/2020/apr/27/public-to-submit-questions-for-uk-covid-19-coronavirus-press-conference (accessed 5 November 2022).

Weaver, M. (2020) Pressure on Dominic Cummings to quit over lockdown breach, *The Guardian*, 22 May, www.theguardian.com/politics/2020/may/22/dominic-cummings-durham-trip-coronavirus-lockdown (accessed 14 August 2020).

Weber, M. (1947 [1922]) *Theory of Social and Economic Organization*, trans. A. R. Anderson and T. Parsons, Oxford: Oxford University Press.

Westen, D. (2007) *The Political Brain: The Role of Emotion in Deciding the Fate of the Nation*, New York: Public Affairs.

White, H. (2022) Why does it matter if a PM lies to parliament? *Financial Times*, 22 April, www.ft.com/content/ee7451b0-5d21-40c8-a3e9-0526923f98a1 (accessed 29 April 2022).

Wood, M., Corbett, J. and Flinders, M. (2016) Just like us: Everyday celebrity politicians and the pursuit of popularity in an age of anti-politics, *The British Journal of Politics and International Relations*, 18: 3, pp. 581–98.

Woodcock, A. (2019) Boris Johnson admits no-deal Brexit will hurt UK while dodging journalists' questions during rambling campaign launch, *The Independent*, 12 June, www.independent.co.uk/news/uk/politics/boris-johnson-no-deal-brexit-damage-tory-leadership-speech-uk-us-a8955361.html (accessed 14 August 2020).

Woodcock, A. (2020) Coronavirus: Government accused of ignoring experts as top advisers absent from press briefings, *The Independent*, 15 June, www.independent.co.uk/news/uk/politics/coronavirus-boris-johnson-press-briefing-downing-street-dominic-raab-a9567446.html (accessed 14 August 2020).

York, C. (2020) How Boris Johnson's 'Stay Alert' message unravelled in 24 calamitous hours, *Huffington Post*, 11 May, www.huffingtonpost.co.uk/entry/coronavirus-government-u-turns-stay-alert_uk_5eb94ac4c5b6d471a12ce8ba (accessed 14 August 2020).

Cambridge Elements ☰

Applied Linguistics

Li Wei

University College London

Li Wei is Chair of Applied Linguistics at the UCL Institute of Education, University College London (UCL), and Fellow of Academy of Social Sciences, UK. His research covers different aspects of bilingualism and multilingualism. He was the founding editor of the following journals: *International Journal of Bilingualism* (Sage), *Applied Linguistics Review* (De Gruyter), *Language, Culture and Society* (Benjamins), *Chinese Language and Discourse* (Benjamins) and *Global Chinese* (De Gruyter), and is currently Editor of the *International Journal of Bilingual Education and Bilingualism* (Taylor and Francis). His books include the *Blackwell Guide to Research Methods in Bilingualism and Multilingualism* (with Melissa Moyer) and *Translanguaging: Language, Bilingualism and Education* (with Ofelia Garcia) which won the British Association of Applied Linguistics Book Prize.

Zhu Hua

University College London

Zhu Hua is Professor of Language Learning and Intercultural Communication at the UCL Institute of Education, University College London (UCL) and is a Fellow of Academy of Social Sciences, UK. Her research is centred around multilingual and intercultural communication. She has also studied child language development and language learning. She is book series co-editor for *Routledge Studies in Language and Intercultural Communication* and *Cambridge Key Topics in Applied Linguistics*, and Forum and Book Reviews Editor of *Applied Linguistics* (Oxford University Press).

About the Series

Mirroring the *Cambridge Key Topics in Applied Linguistics*, this Elements series focuses on the key topics, concepts and methods in Applied Linguistics today. It revisits core conceptual and methodological issues in different subareas of Applied Linguistics. It also explores new emerging themes and topics. All topics are examined in connection with real-world issues and the broader political, economic and ideological contexts.

Cambridge Elements ≡

Applied Linguistics

Elements in the Series